W9-AOQ-024

Windows™ 3.1
First Run

Michele Reader
College of DuPage

QUE
COLLEGE

Windows 3.1 First Run

Copyright © 1993 by Que® Corporation.

All rights reserved. Printed in the United States of America. No part of this book may be used or reproduced in any form or by any means, or stored in a database or retrieval system, without prior written permission of the publisher except in the case of brief quotations embodied in critical articles and reviews. Making copies of any part of this book for any purpose other than your own personal use is a violation of United States copyright laws. For information, address Que College, Prentice Hall Computer Publishing, 201 W. 103rd Street, Indianapolis, IN 46290.

Library of Congress Catalog No.: 93-86097

ISBN: 1-56529-425-4

This book is sold *as is*, without warranty of any kind, either express or implied, respecting the contents of this book, including but not limited to implied warranties for the book's quality, performance, merchantability, or fitness for any particular purpose. Neither Que Corporation nor its dealers or distributors shall be liable to the purchaser or any other person or entity with respect to any liability, loss, or damage caused or alleged to be caused directly or indirectly by this book.

96 95 94   4

Interpretation of the printing code: the rightmost double-digit number is the year of the book's printing; the rightmost single-digit number, the number of the book's printing. For example, a printing code of 93-1 shows that the first printing of the book occurred in 1993.

Screens reproduced in this book were created using Collage Plus from Inner Media, Inc., Hollis, NH.

Windows 3.1 First Run is based on Microsoft Windows 3.1.

Publisher: David P. Ewing

Publishing Director: Mike Miller

Director of Operations and Editing: Chris Katsaropoulos

Book Designer: Amy Peppler-Adams

Indexers: Joy Dean Lee and Suzanne Snyder

Production Team: Angela Bannan, Danielle Bird, Charlotte Clapp, Karen Dodson, Bob LaRoche, Caroline Roop, Amy L. Steed, Tina Trettin, Michelle Worthington

About the Author

Michele Reader is an instructor in the Business and Professional Institute of the College of DuPage. Michele has taught courses on personal computing for five years. She holds a B.A. from North Central College in Naperville, Illinois and has worked as a technical writer and computer trainer for VanKampen Merritt, a division of Xerox. Reader is the author of *MS-DOS First Run*, and also has served as the technical editor of several other books in the *First Run* series, including *Lotus 1-2-3 First Run* and *WordPerfect 5.1 First Run*.

Editorial Director
Carol Crowell

Series Editor
M.T. Cozzola Cagnina

Managing Editor
Sheila B. Cunningham

Production Editor
Jay Lesandrini

Editorial Coordinator

Elizabeth D. Brown

Composed in *ITC Garamond* and *MCPdigital* by Que Corporation

Table of Contents

1 Windows Overview 1

2 Using Window Bars and Dialog Boxes 14

3 Working with Multiple Windows 25

   Testing Your Skills 1 38

4 File Manager Overview 40

5 Using Floppy Disks 50

6 Managing Files and Directories 58

   Testing Your Skills 2 67

7 The Help System 69

8 Using the Print Manager 77

9 Using the Control Panel and Creating
   Group Icons 88

   Testing Your Skills 3 101

   Glossary 103

   Index 107

Acknowledgments

Que College is grateful for the assistance provided by reviewers Jean Insinga, Middlesex Community-Technical College, and James F. Higgins, Moraine Valley Community College. A special thanks also is extended to our technical editor, Cynthia D. Hollingsworth, Indiana University-Purdue University at Indianapolis.

Trademarks

All terms mentioned in this book that are known to be trademarks or service marks have been appropriately capitalized. Que cannot attest to the accuracy of this information. Use of a term in this book should not be regarded as affecting the validity of any trademark or service mark.

Microsoft, Microsoft Word for Windows, and Microsoft Excel, are registered trademarks, and Microsoft Windows is a trademark of Microsoft Corporation. IBM is a registered trademark of International Business Machines Corporation. WordPerfect is a registered trademark of WordPerfect Corporation. Lotus and 1-2-3 are registered trademarks of Lotus Development Corporation.

Preface

The *First Run* series is designed for the novice computer user who wants to learn the basics of a software application as quickly as possible.

First Run combines practical explanations of new concepts and hands-on steps and exercises to build proficiency quickly. Each *First Run* is organized into an average of ten teaching units. Each teaching unit teaches an important skill set. The objectives that make up each teaching unit build on one another section by section. Within the section are steps for performing the function or using the feature, plus an exercise to build your skills. Definitions of new terms and notes on working more effectively also are included.

First Run also offers "Testing Your Skills" sections to enable an instructor to evaluate progress. A glossary of terms is included in every book.

Each section in a unit takes an average of 15 minutes to complete. Because each exercise is tied directly to the current section, instructors can instantly determine a student's progress before continuing to the next section.

An *Instructor's Resource Disk* is available upon adoption of the textbook. It contains answers to all the exercises in the textbook, as well as suggested lecture notes, additional teaching tips and information, extra optional exercises, completed data files, and other data files used in the course.

The unique combination of features in this concise guide makes *First Run* an ideal textbook for step-by-step teaching now and for easy reference later on. Instructors may mix and match individual textbooks in order to design a custom software applications course.

Look for the following additional titles in the *First Run* series:

BASIC First Run	1-56529-416-5
dBASE III Plus First Run	1-56529-418-1
dBASE IV First Run	1-56529-419-X
Excel for Windows First Run	1-56529-420-3
Introduction to PCs First Run	1-56529-417-3
Lotus 1-2-3 First Run	1-56529-421-1
MS-DOS First Run	1-56529-423-8
Novell NetWare First Run	1-56529-424-6
Word for Windows First Run	1-56529-427-0
WordPerfect 5.1 First Run	1-56529-428-9
WordPerfect 6 First Run	1-56529-429-7
WordPerfect for Windows First Run	1-56529-430-0

For more information call

1-800-428-5331

Conventions Used in This Book

The conventions used in this book have been established to help you learn to use the program quickly and easily. As much as possible, the conventions correspond with those used in the Windows 3.1 program documentation.

In this book, keys pressed in combination are joined by a plus sign: Alt+T. The keys you press and the text you type are printed in **boldfaced type**.

DOS commands, file names, and directory names are written in all capital letters. Options, commands, menu names, and dialog box names are headline style. Direct quotations of words that appear on-screen, including prompts, are printed in a special typeface.

 STEPS The Steps Icon, located in the margin, accompanies a listing of particular steps to follow in order to complete a Windows task, such as copying files.

Windows Overview

Windows has become a very popular software program for PC users. You may have heard people talk about upgrading to Windows or about learning new Windows applications. But what is Windows? Will it really make using a personal computer easier? This unit answers these questions, and gets you started using the Windows program.

What Is Windows?

Windows is a software program that works with DOS (the Disk Operating System) to make the use of your personal computer easier. DOS controls all of the computer elements, including the keyboard, the monitor, the printer and the disk drives. *Disk drives* are used to store software applications, such as word processing or spreadsheet programs, and files, such as letters and spreadsheets created with software applications.

1

Objectives

When you have finished this unit, you will have learned the following:

1.1 To Understand the Advantages of Windows

1.2 To Start Windows

1.3 To Use the Program Manager Window

1.4 To Use the Mouse

1.5 To Use the Minimize, Maximize, and Restore Buttons

1.6 To Exit Windows

DOS uses a *command-line interface*, which requires you to type commands in order to execute various functions such as starting a word processing program, or copying a file. To use DOS efficiently, you must memorize these commands.

Windows, however, is a *graphical user interface*, or *GUI* (pronounced "gooey"), which means that graphical images called *icons* are used to represent programs and files. The GUI makes Windows easier to use than DOS because the need to memorize commands is alleviated. With a GUI, you simply select the icon assigned to the function you want to execute, such as starting your word processing program.

Although Windows graphical user interface makes using a PC easier, you still need to have a basic understanding of DOS in order to perform some tasks such as copying files or creating subdirectories. Using the Windows File Manager makes even these functions less difficult, but because DOS still controls your computer's operations, the Windows File Manager must follow DOS's rules. Basic DOS concepts, such as directory structures and file names are outlined briefly in the units on using the File Manager. This course assumes that you are familiar with DOS and the personal computer keyboard.

1.1 To Understand the Advantages of Windows

There are many advantages to using Windows. Some of these are:

- Windows is easier to learn and use than DOS because with the GUI you don't have to memorize commands.
- Windows makes learning various software programs quicker and easier. Most programs written for Windows use the same commands to perform certain functions, including opening, closing, and saving files, as well as printing. Your knowledge of these functions can be quickly transferred between programs.

- Windows enables you to open more than one program at a time. For example, while you are working in a word processing program, you can open a file in your spreadsheet program to check some numbers that you want to include in the word processing document.

- In many Windows applications, you can open more than one document at a time. For example, you can have three spreadsheet files open simultaneously in order to quickly view data in each of them.

- Windows enables you to copy information from one file to another. You can copy part of one document to another document within the same program, and you can even copy information between different types of programs. For example, if you type a letter in a word processing program, you can copy information from a spreadsheet into your letter.

1.2 To Start Windows

If Windows does not appear on-screen when you turn on the computer, type **win** at the C:\> prompt and press ⏎Enter to start Windows.

If Windows doesn't start, it is probably because Windows can't locate the program from your current directory. See your instructor for information on starting the Windows program.

If your PC displays a menu when you turn it on, type the number or letter which corresponds to the Windows option.

After you have started the Windows program, the Program Manager window appears on-screen. The following section discusses in greater detail how to use the Program Manager.

1.3 To Use the Program Manager Window

The Program Manager window is the starting point for the Windows program (see fig. 1.1). It is from this window that you select the software applications you want to use. The area behind the Program Manager window (and all windows) is called the *Desktop*. Take time to familiarize yourself with the components of this window because these same components are found in windows throughout the entire Windows program.

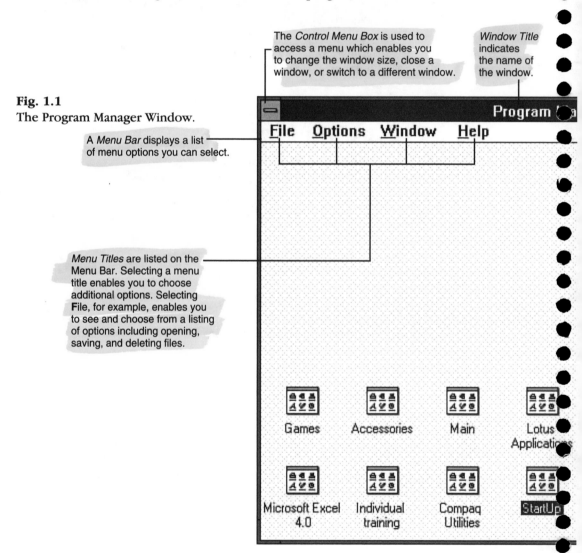

The *Control Menu Box* is used to access a menu which enables you to change the window size, close a window, or switch to a different window.

Window Title indicates the name of the window.

Fig. 1.1
The Program Manager Window.

A *Menu Bar* displays a list of menu options you can select.

Menu Titles are listed on the Menu Bar. Selecting a menu title enables you to choose additional options. Selecting **File**, for example, enables you to see and choose from a listing of options including opening, saving, and deleting files.

The *Title Bar* displays the name of the
active document in that window.

Minimize Button shrinks the active window
to an icon at the bottom of the screen.

Maximize Button expands the active window
to cover the entire screen.

ager

When you move the mouse on your desk, the
Mouse Pointer moves on your screen. Use the
mouse pointer arrow to point to various items
on the window so that they can be selected.

Icons are pictorial representations of a
command, program, or document. The icons
shown here are called *Group Icons*. A Group
icon organizes a collection of software
programs. For example, the Applications icon
may contain both word processing and
spreadsheet programs.

PFS:
pplications

Word for
Windows 2.0

Collage
Complete

The *Window Border* identifies
the edges of the window.

An *Icon Label* names the icon.

5

Exercise 1: Identifying Window Components

From the Program Manager window, use the mouse to point to the following window components.

- Control menu box
- Maximize button
- Main icon
- Window title
- Options menu title

1.4 To Use the Mouse

You can use either a mouse or the keyboard to make selections in Windows, but generally, it is quicker and easier to use the mouse. Using a mouse takes some practice, but as you become more proficient, you will discover that using a mouse can be quick and easy. Although this book assumes that you are using a mouse, in instances where using the keyboard is as convenient as a mouse, the appropriate keystrokes are listed.

In this section, you learn how to use the mouse to

- Open and close windows.
- Move objects.
- Resize a window.
- Exit the Windows program.

 STEPS   Selecting an icon with the mouse requires two steps:

1. Slide the mouse across your desk or mouse pad to move the pointer arrow to the desired location on-screen. If you run out of room on your desk before the arrow is correctly positioned, simply pick up the mouse and move it over, then set it back on your desk, and continue sliding it until the pointer arrow is touching the object you want to select.

2. Click the left mouse button to select the object.

In Windows, the left mouse button is used to make selections. When you hold the mouse with your right hand, use your index finger to click the left mouse button.

If you are left-handed, see the section "Changing Mouse Settings" in Unit 9 to learn how to switch the left and right mouse buttons. Switching the buttons enables you to operate the mouse with your left hand and use your left index

6

finger to click the correct button for making selections. When this book refers to the left mouse button, think of it as whichever button you press with your index finger.

Opening a Window

To open a window, follow these steps:

1. Position the mouse pointer arrow so that it touches the icon you want to select.

2. Double-click by pressing the left mouse button quickly two times to open the window.

 If you discover that you are double-clicking too quickly or too slowly, refer to the section "To Change Mouse Settings" in Unit 9 to learn how to change the mouse setting for the speed of double-clicks.

Closing a Window

To close a window, follow these steps:

1. Move the mouse pointer to the control menu box in the upper-left corner of the window.

2. Double-click the left mouse button.

Moving Icons and Windows

You can move icons and windows to different locations by using a technique called *dragging and dropping*.

To move an icon or a window, follow these steps:

1. Position the mouse pointer arrow on the icon or window you want to move. To move a window, you must point to the window's title bar.

2. Press and hold down the left mouse button.

3. While holding down the left mouse button, slide the mouse across your desk to *drag* the icon or window to its new location.

4. Once you have repositioned the icon or window, release the mouse button. This *drops* the icon in its new position.

Resizing a Window Using the Mouse

You can change the size of a window by using the dragging and dropping technique on a window's borders.

 STEPS

To resize a window, follow these steps:

1. Move the mouse pointer to one of the window's borders. The pointer arrow changes to a two-headed arrow when it touches a window's border (see fig. 1.2).

Two-headed arrow

Fig. 1.2
Resizing a window.

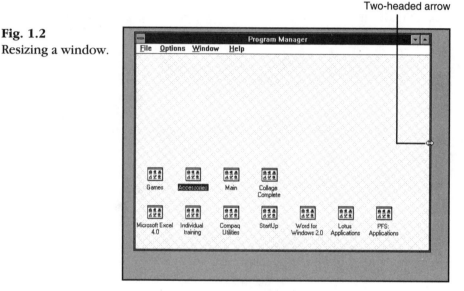

2. Press and hold down the left mouse button.

3. Move the mouse pointer to make the window larger or smaller.

4. When the window is the size you want, release the mouse button.

 STEPS

To change both the length and the width of a window at the same time, use the following steps:

1. Position the mouse pointer at a corner of the window. The pointer arrow changes to a diagonal, two-headed arrow.

2. Drag the corner of the window to change the length and the width at the same time.

3. When the window is the size you want, release the left mouse button.

Exercise 2: Practicing Mouse Skills

In this exercise, you practice using the mouse to move windows and icons, to open and close windows, and to resize windows by dragging their borders.

1. Move several of the group icons to new locations in the Program Manager window by using the dragging and dropping technique.

2. Open the Accessories window and drag it to different locations within the Program Manager window.

3. Practice resizing the Accessories window by dragging its border. Resize it several times.

4. When you have finished, close the Accessories window by double-clicking the control menu box.

1.5 To Use the Minimize, Maximize, and Restore Buttons

In addition to using the mouse to resize a window, you can use the minimize and maximize buttons, located at the top right of each window. (Refer to fig. 1.1 to see the location of these buttons.)

The Minimize Button

When you are working with several documents at one time, the screen can become cluttered. By using the Minimize button (located at the top-right corner of each window), you can clear documents from the screen without closing them. When you click the Minimize button, the active window is changed to an icon which is displayed at the bottom of the screen.

The advantage to minimizing a window instead of closing it, is that when minimized, the window remains loaded in the computer's *memory*. The memory is the temporary work area used by the computer whenever you start a program or open a file. Think of memory as your desktop. You pull files out of a file drawer (the disk drive) and put them on your desk (the memory) to work on them. Information still in the computer's memory when you exit the Windows program or turn off your computer is deleted. For this reason, it is necessary to save files to a *disk*, which is your permanent storage area.

STEPS
To minimize a window, simply click the Minimize button when that window is active. Once a file is minimized, you can quickly access it by double-clicking on its icon instead of having to load a software program into memory and then open the file.

> **! TIP** Make sure you double-click on the *minimized* icon, not the original program icon. If you double-click the original program icon, you will open a duplicate session of that application.

There are three main types of icons you encounter when using Windows. It is important to understand the differences between the three. See figure 1.3 for examples of these icons.

- A *group icon* appears in the Program Manager window. It contains icons used to start various programs. Examples of group icons include Games and Accessories.

- A *program-item* icon represents a program that you have on your computer. These icons are located in a group window. Examples of program-item icons include Solitaire and Write.

- *Application icons* appear at the bottom of your desktop when you have opened and minimized a program or file. For example, if you are creating a document in Write and click the minimize button, the icon that appears at the bottom of your desktop is an application icon.

Fig. 1.3
Windows icons.

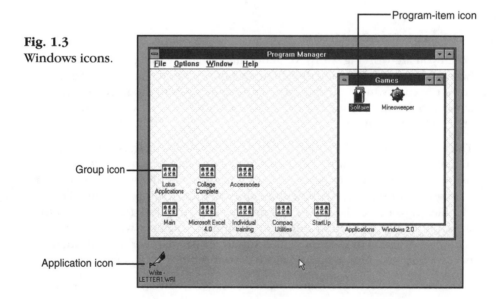

10

Exercise 3: Using the Minimize Button

The following exercise illustrates the advantage of using the Minimize button.

1. Open the Accessories icon.

2. Open the Write program by double-clicking its icon.

3. Click the minimize button.

   The Write icon appears on the bottom-left side of your desktop, outside of the Program Manager window.

4. Close the Accessories window.

5. Double-click the minimized Write icon to reopen it.

6. Because the Write window is minimized and remains in memory, you can still open it without having to first open the Accessories group icon, and then the Write program icon. This is the major advantage of minimizing a file.

Maximizing and Restoring a Window

The Maximize button is located to the right of the Minimize button, and is used to make the window larger so that it fills the entire screen.

To maximize and to restore a window, follow these steps:

1. Click the Maximize button (located to the right of the Minimize button) to enlarge the window to full-screen view.

   When the window is maximized, a button with two arrows appears in the top-right corner of the window. This is the *Restore* button.

2. Click the Restore button to return the window to its previous size.

1.6 To Exit Windows

To exit Windows, follow these steps:

1. Double-click the Control Menu Box in the Program Manager window.

2. A dialog box appears displaying the following prompt: `This will end your Windows session.`

3. Choose OK. If the OK button is highlighted, you can just press `↵Enter`.

11

Exercise 3: Using the Mouse to Resize, Minimize, and Maximize windows

In this exercise, you resize windows by using the mouse; Minimize, Maximize and Restore windows; and exit the Windows program.

1. Open the Main Icon.

2. Resize the window so that it takes up most of the screen.

3. Now make the window smaller, using a corner of the border.

4. Close this window.

5. Using the dragging and dropping technique, move all of the icons to the top of the Program Manager window. Next, move all of the icons to the bottom.

6. Minimize the Program Manager window.

7. Open the minimized Program Manager icon, and maximize the window.

8. Restore the window to its previous size.

9. Exit the Windows program.

10. Restart the Windows program.

Unit Summary

This unit presented a brief overview of Windows, listed several advantages to using Windows, and identified the components of a window. You learned how to use the mouse to open and close a window, to move objects, to resize a window, and to exit the Windows program. You also learned how to use the Minimize and Maximize buttons.

New Terms

To check your knowledge of the new terms in this unit, consult the glossary at the end of this book.

- Application icon
- Desktop
- Disk
- Graphical User Interface (GUI)
- Group icon
- Icons
- Memory
- Program-item icon

2

Using Window Bars and Dialog Boxes

Objectives

When you finish this unit, you will have learned the following:

2.1 To Use the Scroll Bars

2.2 To Use the Menu Bar

2.3 To Use Dialog Boxes

This unit covers several key elements of using Windows, including scroll bars, menu bars, and the dialog boxes. You use all of these components throughout Windows, whether you are working in Program Manager, using various Windows applications, or managing your files. Learning these essential elements enables you to become more proficient in your everyday Windows tasks.

2.1 To Use the Scroll Bars

Scroll Bars appear in a window when there is more information in the window than can be displayed on-screen. Figure 2.1 shows the Program Manager window when group icons have been moved off the top right corner. You can still see part of the icon in the upper-right corner of the window, but most of it has been moved out of view.

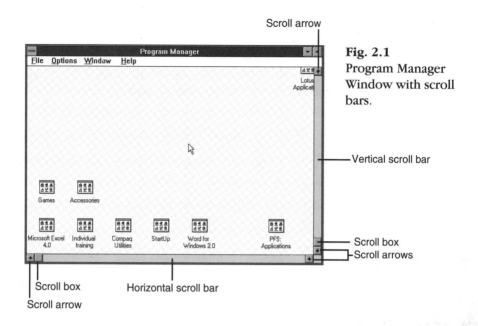

Scroll arrow

Fig. 2.1
Program Manager
Window with scroll
bars.

Vertical scroll bar

Scroll box
Scroll arrows

Scroll box   Horizontal scroll bar

Scroll arrow

Notice that the scroll bars appear along the right side and bottom of the
window. *Scroll arrows* appear on each side of the scroll bar. A *scroll box* also
appears. The scroll box shows your relative position in the window. In figure
2.1, the scroll box is at the bottom of the vertical scroll bar and on the left side
of the horizontal scroll bar. This indicates that you are at the bottom left edge
of the window.

To use the scroll bar to display more of a window, follow these steps:

STEPS

1. Position the cursor on the scroll arrow that points in the direction you
   want to move.

2. Click the left mouse button to move the window in that direction.

3. To move a greater distance than the arrows enable, you can drag the
   scroll box to a different location in the scroll bar, or you can click the
   scroll bar itself to move to that location in the window.

> If you don't see information in a window that should be there, look
> for scroll bars. Scroll the screen, and the information you are looking
> *TIP*   for should appear.

15

Exercise 1: Using the Scroll Bars

This exercise gives you practice using the scroll bars.

1. Drag several icons from the Program Manager window off the top right border of the window. You will still be able to see the bottom of the icons. Your screen should be similar to the one shown in figure 2.1.

2. Position the mouse pointer on the right scroll arrow of the horizontal bar. Click this arrow to move the screen until the scroll box moves all the way to the right. The screen moves to the left, and you can see the bottom of the icons that you moved out of view.

3. Drag the vertical scroll box to the top of the scroll bar. The screen moves up, revealing the icons that you moved.

4. Open the Accessories Group icon.

5. Resize the window, dragging the bottom right corner up and to the left until you see a vertical scroll bar. The window should look like the one shown in figure 2.2.

Fig. 2.2
Accessories
Window with a
scroll bar.

6. Move the window up and down by clicking in different locations along the vertical scroll bar.

7. Close the Accessories group window.

2.2 To Use the Menu Bar

A *Menu Bar* is displayed along the top of many windows. The Menu bar enables you to select various menus in order to perform operations including:

- Opening, printing, and deleting files.
- Editing and formatting documents.
- Accessing the Help system.

This section provides general information about using menus. Specific menu functions are covered in later units. Figure 2.3 shows the Menu bar in the Program Manager window.

Fig. 2.3
The Program Manager Window menu bar.

Follow these steps to display a pull-down menu in a menu bar: *STEPS*

1. Point to the menu title you want to select.

2. Click once with the left mouse button.

> You can also use the keyboard to display a pull-down menu. Press [Alt] (located next to the space bar), and then type the underlined letter in the title of the option you want to select. For example, to see the File menu, type [Alt]+[F].
> *TIP*

When you are instructed to use a menu in this book, the text lists the menu option, such as **File Open**. Use the mouse to click **File**, then **Open**, or press [Alt] and the bolded letter.

After you have selected a menu title, the menu for that option is displayed. Figure 2.4 shows the File menu for the Program Manager window.

Fig. 2.4
The File Menu.

Notice in figure 2.4 that some of the menu options are displayed in dark type, while others are a lighter shade. Shaded menu options are not available for use. In the File menu in figure 2.4, the Move and Copy options cannot be selected because there is not a file open to be moved or copied.

To select an option from a menu, follow these steps: *STEPS*

1. Position the mouse pointer arrow on the option you want.

2. Click the left mouse button to select the option.

> You can also use the keyboard to select a menu option by typing the underlined letter, or using the arrow keys to highlight the option you want and then pressing [↵Enter].
> *TIP*

STEPS If you opened the wrong menu, you can display a different menu by following these steps:

1. Position the mouse pointer arrow over the menu title you want to select.

2. Click the left mouse button.

 You can use the ⬅ and ➡ to display a menu to the right or left of the one currently on your screen.

TIP

 STEPS To close a menu without selecting an option, follow these steps:

1. Position the mouse pointer arrow outside the menu.

2. Click the left mouse button.

 To close a menu using the keyboard, press Esc twice.

TIP

Exercise 2: Using Menus

Complete the following exercise to practice using menus.

1. From the Program Manager window, open the Help menu.

2. Select the menu option How to Use Help.

3. Close the How to Use Help window by double-clicking the Control Menu Box.

4. Display the Window pull-down menu.

5. Display the Options menu by using ⬅ to move to this window.

6. Close the Options menu without selecting an item.

2.3 To Use Dialog Boxes

Dialog boxes appear in a window when the Windows program needs more information from you in order to execute a command. To open a file, for example, you need to enter the file name. A dialog box enables you to enter this information. Dialog boxes may contain the following boxes and buttons:

- Text boxes
- List boxes

- Drop-down list boxes
- Check boxes
- Option buttons
- Command buttons

This section explains how to use each of these components. After you have learned how to use each of these components, you can easily navigate any dialog box in the Windows program.

Text Boxes

When a text box appears, you need to type additional information such as a file name. Figure 2.5 shows the **File Open** dialog box which contains a text box.

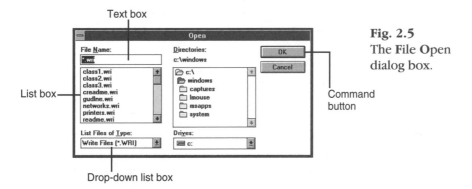

Fig. 2.5
The File Open dialog box.

To enter information in a text box, follow these steps:

1. If the information in the text box is highlighted, you can start typing the necessary information which replaces the highlighted text.

2. If the information is not highlighted, position the mouse pointer in the box. Notice that the pointer arrow turns into an I-beam pointer.

3. Double-click the left mouse button to highlight the text within the box. Type the new information.

4. If there is no text in the box, position the mouse pointer in the box and click the mouse button once to select it.

5. If you want to change or insert only a few letters in the text box, follow these instructions:

    a. Position the I-beam pointer where you want to insert new information.

19

b. Click the left mouse button once.

c. You see a blinking line at the point where you clicked the mouse. This is called the *insertion point*. Any text that you type is inserted to the right of this point.

d. To delete a character to the right of the insertion point, press (Del).

e. To delete a character to the left of the insertion point, press (◆Backspace).

List Boxes

A list box appears to give you a choice of options, such as a list of file names to be entered into a text box (see fig. 2.5).

 STEPS   To select an item displayed in a list box, follow these steps:

1. Position the mouse pointer arrow on the option you want.

2. Click the left mouse button.

   The selected option appears in the text box.

Drop-down List Boxes

A drop-down list box displays only one line until you click the arrow next to the box. After you have clicked the arrow, a list of choices appears. See figure 2.6 for an example of the drop-down list box.

Fig. 2.6
A drop-down list
box.

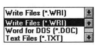

 STEPS   To see a list of options in a drop-down list box, follow these steps:

1. Position the mouse pointer on the arrow next to the drop-down list box.

2. Click the left mouse button once. A list of options appears.

3. If more options are available than those displayed on-screen, a scroll bar appears next to the drop-down list. Scroll through the list to see all of the available options.

4. When you see the option you want to select, position the mouse pointer on that option, and click the left mouse button.

Command Buttons

Command buttons are always labeled with their function. Figure 2.5 contains the OK and Cancel command buttons. You always select OK to execute a dialog box function. The Cancel command button enables you to cancel a box without selecting any of the options. A dialog box may contain other command buttons as well, and each is labeled with its function.

To select a command button, move the pointer arrow to the command button and click the left mouse button. If the command button you want to select is bordered by a dark outline, you can just press ⏎Enter to execute the command.

 STEPS

Exercise 3: Using Text Boxes, List Boxes, Drop-Down List Boxes, and Command Buttons

In this exercise, you practice using several components of a dialog box.

1. Open the Accessories icon from the Program Manager. Next, open the Write program.

2. Select File, and then Open from the Menu bar. A dialog box like the one shown in figure 2.5 appears.

3. Type one of the file names displayed in the list box into the File Name text box. Do not press ⏎Enter.

4. Display the options in the List Files of Type drop-down list box. When you select an option from this list, only files with the selected extension are displayed in the list box.

5. Select the last option, **All Files (*.*)**. You will need to click the down scroll arrow to display this option. All of the files for the selected directory are displayed in the File Name list box.

6. Select the file README.WRI so that it is displayed in the text box.

7. Click the OK command button to open the README.WRI file.

8. Close the Write window by double-clicking the Control menu box.

21

Check Boxes

A check box works as an on/off switch. If an X appears in a check box, the option is turned on. If the box is empty, the option is turned off.

To turn on or turn off an option, follow these steps:

1. Position the mouse pointer on the check box you want to change.

2. Click the left mouse button. If the box is empty, an X is inserted. If the box contains an X, clicking the button removes it. Figure 2.7 shows examples of check boxes.

Option Buttons

When you encounter option buttons in a dialog box, you can choose only one of the available options. The option that you select is indicated by a dark circle within its assigned button (see fig. 2.7).

Fig. 2.7
Check boxes and
Option buttons
for the game
Solitaire.

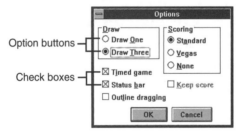

To select an option button, follow these steps:

1. Position the mouse pointer arrow on the button next to the option you want to select.

2. Click the left mouse button. A dark circle appears in the option button.

> One of the options in an option button group must be selected. You cannot deselect an option by clicking on the selected option button; you must make another selection.

Exercise 4: Using Check Boxes and Option Buttons

In this exercise you practice using other dialog box components.

1. Open the Games program group icon, and then the Solitaire icon.

2. When the Menu bar appears, select **G**ame, and then Options.
   The Options dialog box appears.

3. Click the check boxes so that only the following options are selected:

   • Timed game

   • Status bar

   Your dialog box should look like the one shown in figure 2.7.

4. Select the following options in the Options dialog box for the Solitaire game:

   • Draw Three

   • Standard Scoring

5. When you have made these changes, click OK to execute your changes.

6. Close the Solitaire window, then the Games window.

Exercise 5: Using the Print Dialog Box

In this exercise, you extend your knowledge of dialog boxes by learning how to use the Print dialog box.

1. Open the Accessories Group icon, and then the Write program.

2. Select the **F**ile menu option, and then **P**rint. The Print dialog box appears (see figure 2.8).

 NOTE Your dialog box may vary slightly, depending on the printer you are using.

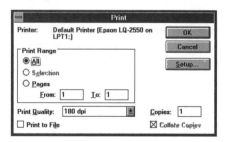

Fig. 2.8
The Print dialog box.

3. Select the following options in the Print dialog box:

Option:	Set to:
Print Range	Pages From 1 To 5
Print Quality	Change this to a different option that appears in the drop down list box
Copies	2
Print to File	Make sure that this box is not checked

4. After you have selected these options, your dialog box should look similar to the one shown in figure 2.9.

Fig. 2.9
The Print dialog
box with new
settings.

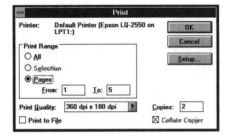

5. Choose Cancel so that nothing prints.

6. Close the Write program, and then close the Accessories window.

Unit Summary

In this unit, you learned how to use the scroll bars to display additional information in a window. You learned how to use the menu bar and how to select options from a menu. You also learned how to use a dialog box, including all of the various boxes and buttons you may see within one.

New Terms

To check your knowledge of the new terms in this unit, consult the glossary at the end of this book.

- Dialog boxes
- Insertion point
- Menu bar
- Scroll bars

Working with Multiple Windows

3

One of the major advantages of using Windows is that you can have different Windows applications open at the same time. For instance, you can work in word processing and graphics applications while you have a spreadsheet document open. Having many windows open can be confusing, however, until you learn how to deal with multiple windows. This unit discusses methods for using multiple windows.

3.1 To Arrange Group Windows on Your Desktop

The Window option appears in the menu bar of the Program Manager window. This option enables you to arrange open windows by *cascading* or *tiling* them. These methods, explained in detail in the following sections, arrange open windows so that it is easy to locate and work with the ones you want.

When you select the Window option from the Program Manager window, it arranges only *group windows*, which are windows that you open directly from the Program Manager. Some examples of group windows are the

Objectives

When you finish this unit, you will have learned the following:

3.1 To Arrange Group Windows on Your Desktop

3.2 To Use the Task List

3.3 To Move between Open Windows

3.4 To Use the Clipboard to Copy and Move Information between Windows

Accessories window, the Main window, and the Games window. Group windows contain *program-item icons* which are used to start applications.

The Window option does not arrange files that you open within an application. To learn how to cascade or tile application windows, see the section "To Use the Task List" later in this unit.

Cascading Windows

When you cascade open windows, they are arranged diagonally, one on top of another, so that the title bar of each window is displayed. The top (or front) window of the stack is fully visible as you can see in figure 3.1. The window that is currently active when you select the cascade option will always be on top.

Fig. 3.1
Cascaded windows.

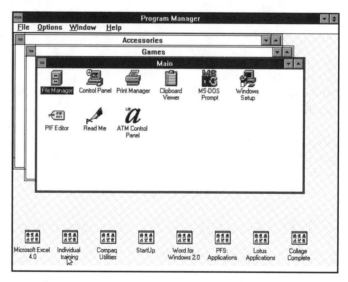

 STEPS To cascade windows, select **Window Cascade** from the Program Manager menu bar. The open windows are cascaded.

Tiling Windows

Selecting the Tile option from the **Window** menu arranges all of the open windows on your screen side by side, each in an individual window. The size of each window depends on how many windows are open. If you have three open windows, you can see all three when they are tiled, and all are the same size. Figure 3.2 shows three tiled windows.

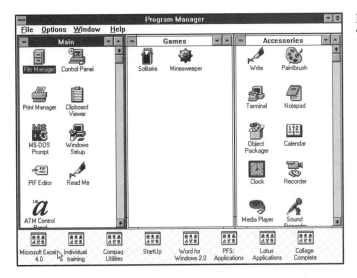

Fig. 3.2
Tiled windows.

To tile all open windows, select Window Tile from the Program Manager menu bar. All open windows are tiled. **STEPS**

Arranging Icons

Icons sometimes become scattered within a window, and can even be located out of your view but still be in the window. You can rearrange icons by either dragging and dropping as you did in Unit 1, or by using the Arrange Icons option to "clean up" your screen.

To use the Arrange Icons option, choose Window from the Program Manager menu bar, and then choose Arrange Icons. All of the icons are organized into rows at the bottom of the window. **STEPS**

 TIP If you Cascade or Tile your windows, the Program Group icons are arranged along the bottom of the Program Manager window at the same time. You do not have to select the Arrange Icons option separately.

Exercise 1: Arranging Group Windows and Icons

Practice arranging your Group windows by completing the following exercise.

1. Open the following program groups in the order given:

    Accessories

    Games

    Main

27

2. From the Program Manager menu bar, choose **Window Cascade**. Your screen should look similar to the one shown in figure 3.1.

3. Now tile these windows. The open windows are tiled as shown in figure 3.2.

4. Close one of the tiled windows by double-clicking the Control menu box of that window.

5. Cascade the windows again.

6. Close the two group windows.

7. Move the group icons to different locations in the Program Manager window.

8. Use the Arrange Icons option to reorganize these icons.

3.2 To Use the Task List

The Task List is a window that lists all of the *application windows* that are open. An application window contains a program that is currently running. For example, a window containing an open Write file or an open Paintbrush document is an application window. This section introduces Task List which enables you to do the following:

- Switch to a different window.
- Close a window.
- Cascade and tile application windows.
- Arrange application icons.

Opening the Task List

STEPS

To open the Task List, double-click any part of the desktop that is not covered with a window. If you cannot see the desktop, press and hold down Ctrl, and then press Esc. Figure 3.3 shows the Task List window.

The Task List displays all open application windows on your desktop. A scroll bar appears when more application windows are open than can be displayed in one Task List window. Use the scroll arrows to display the names of additional open application windows. Notice in figure 3.3 that Task List option buttons are displayed at the bottom of the window.

Fig. 3.3
The Task List
window.

Switching to a Different Window

To activate a different window, you can double-click the name of the window
you want, or use the *Switch To* option button in the Task List.

To use the Switch To option button, follow these steps:

1. In the Task List, highlight the name of the window you want to
   activate. Use the scroll bars to locate this window if necessary.

2. Click the Switch To option button, or press [Alt]+[S].

3. The newly-activated window moves to the top of the window stack.

Ending a Task

To close an application window from the Task List, use the End Task
command button.

To use the End Task command button, follow these steps:

1. Highlight the name of the application window you want to close.

2. Click the End Task command button, or press [Alt]+[E].

3. The selected window closes.

Canceling the Task List

To exit the Task List window without selecting an option, just click the Cancel
command button, or press [Esc].

Exercise 2: Using Some Features of Task List

In this exercise, you practice opening and closing the Task List window, canceling a task, and ending a task.

1. Open the following windows:

    Games, then Solitaire

    Accessories, then Write, Paintbrush, and Cardfile

 TIP After you open a program in the Accessories window, you may not be able to see the other program-item icons. Click on any part of the Accessories window once and it moves to the front of your screen. You can continue selecting the other programs you want to open. If you can't see any part of the Accessories window, you need to use Task List to activate it.

2. Open the Task List window.

 NOTE Notice that the Accessories and Games windows are not listed in Task List. Task List displays only open Application windows. Because Accessories and Games are Group windows, they reside in the Program Manager window.

3. Use the Switch To button to activate the Write window.

4. Close the Solitaire window using the Task List.

You will be using these open Application windows in exercise 3.

Cascading and Tiling Open Windows

The cascade and tile options arrange windows in Task List just as they do in the Window menu; however, in Task List, the cascade and tile options only arrange open Application windows.

 STEPS To cascade Application windows from the Task List window, follow these steps:

1. Display Task List by pressing Ctrl + Esc.

2. Select the Cascade option button, or press Alt + C.

3. All of the open Application windows are cascaded as shown in figure 3.4.

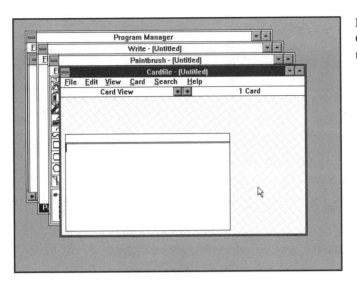

Fig. 3.4
Cascaded Application windows.

To tile Application windows from the Task List window, follow these steps:

1. Press Ctrl + Esc to display the Task List.

2. Select the Tile option button, or press Alt + T.

3. All of the open Application windows are tiled as shown in figure 3.5.

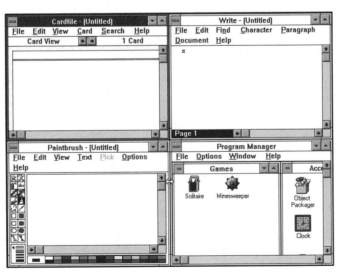

Fig. 3.5
Tiled Application windows.

Arranging Application Icons

In Unit 1, you learned that minimizing a window instead of closing it enables that window's application to remain loaded in your computer's memory, while the Windows Program displays that application as an icon at the bottom of your screen. The Arrange Icons option in the Task List is used to arrange these *application icons* so that they are lined up in a row along the bottom of your desktop.

 STEPS

To arrange icons from the Task List window, follow these steps.

1. Press Ctrl+Esc to display the Task List.

2. Select Arrange Icons.

3. All of the minimized icons are rearranged at the bottom of your desktop.

 NOTE If your Program Manager window is maximized, you will not be able to see the application icons on your desktop.

Exercise 3: Cascading and Tiling Application Windows, and Arranging Application Icons

In this exercise you practice using Task List to cascade and tile Application windows, as well as to arrange Application icons.

1. Use Task List to Cascade your open application windows.

2. Tile your open application windows.

3. Minimize the following windows by clicking the minimize button in the top-right corner of each window:

   - Cardfile
   - Write
   - Paintbrush

4. Each of these windows now appears as an icon at the bottom of your screen, with the application name and file name listed. In this case, you haven't created any files with the applications, so all of the file names are listed as "Untitled."

5. Move the icons around on your screen, so that they aren't lined up along the bottom.

6. From Task List, select Arrange Icons. The icons are lined up at the bottom of your desktop.

7. Double-click on each of these icons to reopen it before going on to the next section.

3.3 To Move between Open Windows

Although you can have many windows open on your desktop, you can only work in one window at a time. The window you are currently working in is called the *active window*.

To make a window active, just click any part of that window. The window moves to the front of your desktop. If all of the open windows are tiled, the active window doesn't move; instead, the title bar and border of the active window are highlighted.

If you can't see any part of the window you want to activate, you must cascade or tile the windows, or use the Task List Switch To option in order to activate a specific window.

Exercise 4: Activating Windows

In this exercise, you practice activating different windows.

1. Tile the open windows on your screen.

2. Click in the Cardfile window to activate it. Notice that the title bar and border are highlighted in this window. If you start typing, the text is entered into this window.

3. Now click the Write window.

4. Cascade the windows using the Task List.

   The active window moves to the front of the stack of cascaded windows. Its title bar and border are highlighted.

5. Click any part of the Paintbrush window. This window moves to the front of the stack.

6. After you have moved several windows to the front, you may not be able to see the title bar of the window you want to select. Cascade or tile the windows so you can see the title bars and can select the window you want.

7. Close all of the open windows, except for the Program Manager.

3.4 To Use the Clipboard to Copy and Move Information between Windows

Windows applications enable you to copy or move text or graphics to different locations in the same document, or from one document to another. This can be useful if you have numbers from a spreadsheet application that you want to copy to a letter in a word processing application.

The *Clipboard* is a section of Windows memory that stores the information you want to copy or move to another document. To move information into the Clipboard, you either *cut* or *copy* it. If you *cut* text or a graphical image, it is deleted from the original document and moved to the Clipboard. *Copying* the information leaves the text or graphical image in the original document, and places a copy of it on the Clipboard. Information that has been cut or copied to the Clipboard can be placed into a document by *pasting* it there.

The Clipboard only holds the most recent information you have cut or copied—when you cut or copy again, the existing information on the Clipboard is replaced with the new information. You can continue pasting the information from the Clipboard into different locations until you either cut or copy again, or end your Windows session. Ending a Windows session erases all information in the Clipboard.

Viewing the Contents of the Clipboard

STEPS

Normally, the Clipboard works in the background and you do not see it. If you want to see the contents of your Clipboard, follow these steps:

1. Open the Main group icon.

2. Open the Clipboard Viewer program-item icon.

3. A window appears, showing the contents of the Clipboard. If you have not cut or copied text during this Windows session, the Clipboard is empty.

4. Close the Clipboard Viewer window by double-clicking in the Control menu box.

Selecting Text to Copy or Move

STEPS

To copy or move information from one document to another, you must first select the text or graphics you want to copy or move. Follow these steps to select text in a document:

The method used for selecting graphics varies depending upon which application program you are using. For instructions on selecting graphics in a particular application, refer to the user's manual for that application.

1. Open the document from which you want to copy or cut information.

2. Select the text you want to copy or cut by moving the mouse pointer arrow to the beginning of the text. Note that the mouse pointer turns into a large letter I, called an *I-beam*.

3. Hold down the left mouse button, and drag through the text you want to select. The text you drag is highlighted. See figure 3.6 for an example of selected text and an I-beam pointer.

After selecting text to cut or copy, you must immediately select the Cut or Copy command. If you click in another location, the text is deselected.

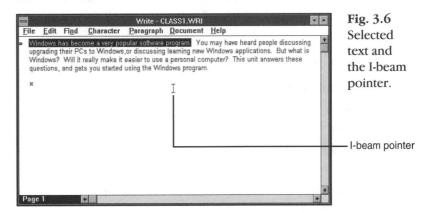

Fig. 3.6 Selected text and the I-beam pointer.

Cutting or Copying Text

After selecting the desired text, you are ready to cut or copy it.

To cut or copy text, follow these steps:

1. After you have selected the text you want, choose Edit from the menu bar.

2. To cut the text, choose Cut from the Edit menu.

   The text is deleted from the current document and placed on the Clipboard.

3. To copy the text, choose Copy from the Edit menu.

   The text is copied to the Clipboard.

4. To paste the text, open the document to which you want to paste (if it is not already open). Find the location in the document where you want to paste the text and click the left mouse button.

5. From the menu bar, choose Edit, then **Paste**. The text is pasted from the clipboard into the document.

Exercise 5: Using the Clipboard to Copy Text

Complete the following exercise to practice copying text from one document to another.

1. Open the Write application, and type the following text into a new file:

   This graphic symbol illustrates the relationship between sales in 1991 and 1992.

2. Select this text.

3. From the menu bar, choose Edit, and then Copy.

4. Open the Paintbrush application.

5. Click the **abc** icon on the left side of the Paintbrush window. This enables you to enter text into the document.

6. Click the mouse pointer (which is now an I-beam) inside of the Paintbrush window.

7. Choose the menu option Edit, **Paste**. This sentence is pasted in your Paintbrush document.

8. Close the Paintbrush window. Choose **No** when prompted to save the current changes.

9. Close the Write window. Choose **No** when prompted to save the current changes.

10. Close the Accessories window.

11. Open the Main program group, then Clipboard Viewer. The text you copied should be displayed in this window.

12. Close the Clipboard Viewer, then the Main window.

Unit Summary

This unit discussed working with multiple open windows. You learned how to cascade and tile both group and application windows, and how to arrange icons. You learned how to switch between open windows, and you learned how to copy text from one window to another.

New Terms

To check your knowledge of the new terms in this unit, consult the glossary at the end of this book.

- Active window
- Application windows
- Clipboard
- Copy
- Group windows

Testing Your Skills 1

(Units 1-3)

The following exercise is provided for you as a self-check to make sure that you understand the concepts and procedures presented to this point. If you have forgotten how to do something, refer back to the sections of this book which pertain to that subject.

1. Open the following group icons:

   > Accessories
   > Main
   > Games

2. Maximize the Program Manager window.

3. Cascade the windows.

4. Select the Accessories window.

5. Resize this window so that it covers most of the screen.

6. Resize this again so that it displays only three icons.

7. Use the scroll bars to display all of the icons.

8. Open the following programs:

   > Write
   > Notepad
   > Calculator

9. Use the Task List to Tile the application windows.

10. Close the following windows by using the Task List:

>   Calculator
>   Notepad
>   Write

11. Maximize the Program Manager window.

12. Close the following windows by using the Control menu box:

>   Main
>   Games
>   Accessories

13. Open the Accessories group icon, then the Write application.

14. Insert the diskette your instructor gives you. It contains several Write documents.

15. Open the file CLASS1.WRI using the menu options **File Open.**

16. Select the first sentence of this document, then choose **Edit Copy.**

17. Open the file CLASS2.WRI.

 Write lets you have only one document open at a time. When you open the second document, the first is closed **NOTE** automatically.

18. Paste the contents of the Clipboard to the end of the first paragraph in the CLASS2.WRI document.

19. Close CLASS2.WRI without saving it.

20. Open the Main group icon, and then the Clipboard Viewer.

21. The sentence you just copied is on the Clipboard. Notice that the copy you made in the previous exercise in Unit 3 is no longer on the Clipboard.

22. Close Clipboard View, then the Main group icon.

23. Close the Accessories window.

24. Exit Windows.

25. Restart the Windows program.

4

File Manager Overview

Objectives

When you finish this unit, you will have learned the following:

4.1 To Understand DOS Terms Related to Windows File Manager

4.2 To Access the File Manager

4.3 To Change to a Different Drive

4.4 To Create a Directory

4.5 To Open and Close a Directory Window

4.6 To Change the Display of a Directory

4.7 To Exit File Manager

If you have worked with DOS, you know how difficult it can be to work with files and subdirectories. Because Windows uses icons to represent directories, subdirectories and files, you actually can see which elements are contained in each directory. This unit introduces you to the Windows File Manager, which enables you to maintain a disk, and to copy, move, and delete your files more easily.

1.1 To Understand DOS Terms Related to Windows File Manager

Before you can completely understand Windows File Manager, you need to be familiar with basic DOS terms. Although Windows enables you to work on your computer without using DOS directly, DOS still controls your files. The rules for naming files and subdirectories, as well as the directory structure itself, are the same whether you are working in Windows or DOS. By reviewing and familiarizing yourself with the terms in Table 4.1, you can make your work with Windows File Manager much easier.

Table 4.1 Basic DOS Terms	
Term	*Definition*
File	A collection of data, such as a letter or spreadsheet, or a program, such as Write or Paintbrush.
File name	A name assigned to files so that they can be identified and accessed. Follow these rules when naming files: • File names must be from 1-8 characters long. • Use only letters or numbers, which makes it easier to remember the name, and avoid using characters that aren't allowed. The following characters cannot be used in a file name: . " / \ [ ] : * < > + = ; , ? • Do not use spaces in file names. • You can use an optional three character extension by typing a period after the file name, and then typing the extension. Some examples of valid file names are: FILE1 LETTER.DOC 70993.WK1
Disk	The storage area for files. A hard disk is generally located inside the computer and cannot be removed. Disk drives are always named with a letter followed by a colon. The hard drive is drive C:. If the hard disk is divided into additional drives, they are labeled D:, E:, F:, etc.
Diskette	A diskette, or *floppy disk*, is a small, removable disk that doesn't store as much information as a hard disk. A diskette is inserted into a *floppy drive*, which is referred to as drive A:. If you have a second floppy drive, it is labeled drive B:.
Directory	A section of the disk which enables you to store related files together so that they are easier to find.

continues

Table 4.1 Continued	
Term	*Definition*
	The *root directory* is the starting point for all directories, and is identified by a backslash (\). From the root directory, you can create many additional *subdirectories* to store files such as spreadsheets or word processing documents. When naming directories, follow the same rules as for files.
Parent directory	The directory immediately above the current directory. The *root directory* is the parent to all directories on your disk. If you create a subdirectory called WORDPROC, for example, and then create a subdirectory to WORDPROC named LETTERS; WORDPROC is the parent to the LETTERS subdirectory.

A good analogy to help you understand disks, directories, and files is to think of your disk drive as a file cabinet which can store a great deal of information. If you just randomly put papers into your filing cabinet, finding a specific document would be very difficult. You must organize your file cabinet by using file folders. This analogy can be easily remembered because Windows uses a file cabinet as the icon for the File Manager.

Your hard disk can be organized in the same way by using directories. Consider the subdirectories of the root directory as the hanging folders in a file drawer. Additional subdirectories are like manila folders within the hanging folders. The individual files are like documents filed within these folders.

4.2 To Access the File Manager

STEPS

To access the File Manager, follow these steps:

1. Open the Main Program group icon.

2. Open the File Manager icon.

3. A window appears showing icons that represent directories and files on your disk.

Figure 4.1 shows an open File Manager window. Familiarize yourself with the components of the File Manager by comparing the labeled components of figure 4.1 with their descriptions in Table 4.2.

Disk drive icon

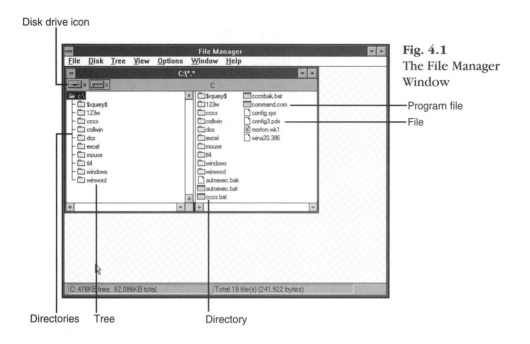

Fig. 4.1
The File Manager
Window

Program file

File

Directories   Tree   Directory

Table 4.2   Components of the File Manager Window

Component	*Description*
Disk drive icons	Represent the disk drives on your computer. The drive icon outlined with a box represents the active drive currently displayed in the window.
Directory	The right side of the window which displays all of the files in the active directory.
Directories	Within a directory, each folder icon represents a subdirectory on the current disk. The first folder, which contains a backslash (\) in its label, is the root directory. The others shown in this figure are subdirectories of the root.
Program file	Program files are applications such as word processing or spreadsheet programs. Program files typically have a .COM or .EXE extension.
File	A file icon represents ordinary files such as word processing or spreadsheet documents.

continues

43

Table 4.2   Continued

Component	Description
Tree	This visual display of your directory structure is located on the left side of the window. The directory structure is referred to as a Tree because directories "branch off" of each other.

4.3 To Change to a Different Drive

STEPS

To display a different drive, click once on the icon that represents the drive you want to see.

Make sure a diskette is in drive A, then select this drive. The contents of your diskette are displayed on-screen.

4.4 To Create a Directory

You may need to create a new directory when loading new software, or you may want to create a new directory to store specific files.

STEPS

To create a new directory, follow these steps:

1. Make sure that the *parent* directory folder is open.

2. Choose File Create Directory.

3. The Create Directory dialog box appears (see fig. 4.2).

Fig. 4.2
The Create
Directory dialog
box.

4. The current directory is identified at the top of the dialog box. The directory you are creating is branched off of the current directory. If you do not want to branch off of the current directory listed, select the Cancel command button. You can then select the correct parent directory and start again with Step 2.

5. In the **N**ame Text box, type a name for the new directory.

6. Choose the OK command button.

7. A directory with the name you entered is created. A folder with this name appears in the tree display of the window.

Exercise 1: Creating a New Directory

Complete this exercise to practice creating a new directory. Your instructor will give you a formatted diskette to use.

1. Insert a formatted diskette into drive A. Change the active drive to A.

2. The new directory will be created off of the root directory. Make sure that the root directory (A:\) folder is highlighted.

3. Select **F**ile C**r**eate Directory.

4. In the text box, type **winclass**.

5. Press ⏎Enter, or choose OK.

6. Notice that the WINCLASS directory is branching off of the root directory.

4.5 To Open and Close a Directory Window

To make it easier to work with several drives and directories at the same time, you can open additional windows to display other drives and directories. After you have finished with a window, it is good practice to close it to keep your screen from becoming too cluttered. The following sections explain how to open and close directory windows.

Opening Additional Directory Windows

You may want to see more than one directory at the same time in order to copy files or to compare the contents of two directories.

To display an additional directory window, follow these steps:

1. Double-click the icon representing the drive you want to display. You can display a different drive, or a second window of the same drive.

2. A second window appears, showing the contents of the selected drive (see fig. 4.3).

Notice in figure 4.3 that the Title Bars on each window identify the contents of the window.

To switch between the windows, click anywhere on the window you want to activate, or press Ctrl + Tab↹.

You can also tile the windows to see both at the same time by selecting **Window Tile**.

Fig. 4.3
A Window display-
ing the contents of
two disk drives.

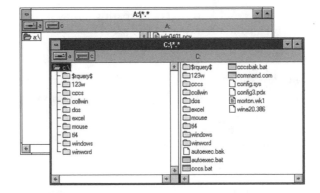

Closing Directory Windows

You can close any additional windows that are open, but one window always stays open. In order to close the last window, you have to close the File Manager program. Closing the File Manager is covered in objective 7.

 STEPS   To close a File Manager window, double-click in the window's Control menu box.

Exercise 2: Opening and Closing Directory Windows

Complete the following exercise to practice opening and closing directory windows.

1. With a window displaying the A drive on-screen, display the contents of your C drive. Your screen should look like figure 4.3.

2. Open an additional window for your C drive. Display the contents of a different subdirectory.

3. Close both C drive windows.

4.6 To Change the Display of a Directory

You can change the way that the File Manager window displays information by using the View option on the Menu Bar. Figure 4.4 shows the View drop-down menu.

The options available in the View menu are described in Table 4.3.

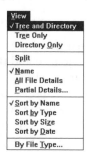

Fig. 4.4
The View menu.

Exercise 3: Changing a Window's Display

Practice changing the way information is displayed in a window by completing the following exercise.

1. Change the open window to display the contents of the WINDOWS subdirectory. This subdirectory is probably on drive C.

2. Display the Tree only.

3. Display the Directory only.

4. Sort by file name.

5. Display all file details.

6. Display Tree and Directory.

7. Move the split in the screen to the left.

8. Select the following partial details to display: size, last modification date.

4.7 To Exit File Manager

To exit the File Manager program, either double-click the File Manager Control menu box, which is located to the left of the title bar, or choose File Exit.

STEPS

Table 4.3 Available Options in the View Menu	
Option	*Description*
Tree and Directory	Displays both the tree structure for the selected drive and for the files in the active subdirectory.
Tree Only	Displays only the tree structure in the window.
Directory Only	Displays only the files in the current directory.
Split	Enables you to change where the screen is divided between the tree and the directory. If you select this option, a black line appears on-screen. Use either the mouse or the arrow keys to move the line to where you want the window to be divided, and then either click the left mouse button or press ⏎Enter.
Name	Displays only the names of the files in the directory list.
All File Details	Displays the file name, file size, date and time created or last modified, and file attributes (whether a file is a hidden, system, archive or read only file).
Partial Details	Enables you to choose which file details you want to display. Check each option that you want, and then select OK.
Sort By Name, Type, Size, Date	Enables you to choose the order of the display of your directory. You can display items sorted by file name, file type (which sorts by extension), file size (largest to smallest), or by the date that the file was saved (newest to oldest).
By File Type	Enables you to select which types of files you want to display, such as directories, program files, or documents.

Unit Summary

In this unit, you reviewed some basic DOS terms before you learned how to use the Windows File Manager to display the directories of different disk drives, to create a new directory, and to open and close a directory window. You also learned how to change the way that the directory is displayed on your screen.

New Terms

To check your knowledge of the new terms in this unit, consult the glossary at the end of this book.

- Directory
- Disk
- Disk drive
- File
- File name
- Parent directory
- Subdirectory

5

Using Floppy Disks

Objectives

When you finish this unit, you will have learned the following:

5.1 To Care for Your Floppy Disks

5.2 To Format a Floppy Disk

5.3 To Make a System Disk

5.4 To Copy a Disk

5.5 To Add a Volume Label to a Disk

Floppy disks, or *diskettes*, are small, removable disks that you use to store files. You can use either a 5 1/4-inch or a 3 1/2-inch diskette, depending on the size of your disk drive. You use floppy disks for many reasons, including saving a backup copy of a file, and transferring information from one computer to another. This unit covers basic information about using diskettes.

5.1 To Care for Your Floppy Disks

Diskettes are fairly durable, but do require some care. To keep your diskettes error-free, follow these guidelines:

- Do not expose diskettes to extreme heat or cold (above 125° or below 50° fahrenheit).
- Never touch an exposed part of a 5 1/4-inch floppy disk.
- Do not carry diskettes through airport security X-ray machines.
- Keep diskettes away from magnetic fields, such as telephones and calculators.
- Do not smoke in the area where you are using a diskette. The smoke can damage it.
- Avoid spilling food or drinks on your diskettes.

- Always store diskettes in a safe place, such as a diskette holder, when not in use.
- Always label your diskettes. This prevents you from erasing information from the wrong diskette.
- When labeling 5 1/4-inch floppy disks, use a felt-tip pen. The pressure of a ball-point pen can damage the disk through the flexible protective coating.

5.2 To Format a Floppy Disk

Formatting a floppy disk prepares it to store files by dividing the diskette into sectors and creating a *File Allocation Table* (FAT) to keep track of the information stored in each sector. Unless you buy preformatted diskettes, you must format each new diskette before you can use it.

⚠️ When you format a diskette, any files currently on the diskette are erased. Be sure to verify that there are no files that you want to keep **WARNING** on a diskette before you format it.

To format a diskette, follow these steps.

1. Insert a diskette into your floppy disk drive.

2. Access Windows File Manager.

3. Choose **Disk** Format Disk. The Format Disk dialog box appears (see fig. 5.1).

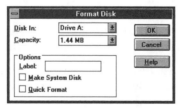

Fig. 5.1
Format Disk dialog box.

4. If necessary, change the drive name containing the diskette by using the **Disk** In drop-down list box.

5. Select the capacity of the diskette you are formatting using the **Capacity** drop-down list box.

NOTE You may notice the **Quick Format** check box. This option is only available if you are reformatting a diskette. It speeds up the formatting process because it does not look for bad sectors on the diskette.

6. Select OK.

7. A confirmation prompt appears, asking you to verify that you have selected the correct disk drive. If the drive is correct, select **Yes**.

8. The computer formats your diskette. After the formatting is complete, a dialog box appears to tell you how much disk space is available, and asks if you want to format another diskette.

9. To format another diskette, choose **Yes**. If you do not want to format another diskette, choose **No**.

 TIP After you have formatted a new diskette, put a label on it. By labeling each formatted diskette, you will know that all diskettes with labels have been formatted, and you will be less likely to reformat a diskette accidentally.

5.3 To Make a System Disk

When your computer *boots*, or starts up, it looks for certain operating system files located in the COMMAND.COM program file. It looks in drive A first, and if no diskette is found, the computer looks for the files on your hard drive.

If the hard disk or one of the files needed to boot has a problem, you may not be able to start your PC. A System Disk is a diskette that contains the files necessary to boot your computer. It is a good idea to create at least one system disk so that you can still boot your computer if you have problems with your hard drive.

If you have two floppy disk drives, use drive A to create the system disk. When the computer boots, it doesn't look at drive B, so if your system disk were to be located there, the computer would not be able to read it.

You can create a system disk when you format a diskette, or you can copy the operating system files to a formatted diskette by using the Disk menu. The following sections discuss both methods for creating a system disk.

Creating a System Disk when Formatting

To create a system disk when you are formatting a diskette, follow these steps:

1. Insert the diskette to be formatted into drive A.

2. From File Manager, choose **Disk Format Disk**.

3. Choose the Disk Drive and Capacity as outlined in the previous section.

4. Choose the **Make System Disk** check box.

5. Choose OK.

6. The diskette is formatted, and the COMMAND.COM program is copied to it.

7. If you want to format another diskette, choose Yes when the dialog box appears. If you do not want to format another diskette, choose No.

Creating a System Disk by Using the Disk Menu

To copy the system files to a formatted diskette, follow these steps:

1. Insert the formatted diskette into drive A.

2. From the File Manager, choose **Disk Make System Disk**.

3. A dialog box appears asking you to confirm that you want to copy the system files onto the diskette. Choose Yes to continue.

4. The COMMAND.COM program file is copied to your diskette.

Exercise 1: Formatting Diskettes and Making System Disks

Complete the following exercise to practice formatting diskettes and making system disks.

1. Insert a diskette to be formatted into the disk drive. If possible do not use the diskette on which you created the WINCLASS subdirectory in Unit 4, because you will copy files to that subdirectory in an exercise in Unit 6.

2. Format the diskette, following the steps in the previous section, "Formatting a Floppy Disk."

3. Choose No when asked if you want to format another.

4. Copy the system files onto this diskette by using the **Disk Make** System Disk menu option.

5. Choose the **No** command button when prompted to format another diskette.

5.4 To Copy a Disk

If you want to copy all of the files from one floppy disk to another, you can use the Copy Disk command. This method creates an identical copy of a *source* diskette (the one you are copying *from*) onto a *destination* diskette (the one you are copying *to*). When you copy diskettes, both must be the same capacity. For example, if the source diskette is a 3 1/2-inch, high density diskette, the destination diskette must also be a 3 1/2-inch high density diskette.

One advantage of using Windows Copy Disk command instead of using the DOS DISKCOPY command is that you don't have to switch back and forth between the source and destination disks. If your disk drive has a capacity higher than 360K, all of the information is copied from the source disk in one step.

⚠ **WARNING** The Copy Disk command erases all of the files on the destination diskette before copying the new information onto it. Be sure that there are no files you want to keep on this diskette before using this command.

 STEPS To copy the files from one diskette to another, follow these steps:

1. From the File Manager, choose **Disk Copy Disk**.

2. A confirmation dialog box appears warning you that all data will be erased from the destination disk. Choose **Yes** to continue.

3. You are prompted to insert the *source* disk. Insert the diskette that you are copying *from*, and click OK.

4. The computer copies the diskette.

5. You are prompted to insert the *destination* disk. Insert the diskette you are copying *to*, and click OK.

6. Windows copies the files from the source diskette onto the destination diskette.

Exercise 2: Copying a Diskette

Practice copying a diskette by completing the steps in this exercise.
Your instructor will provide you with a diskette that has several files.

1. From the File Manager window, choose **Disk Copy Disk**.

2. Copy the diskette provided by your instructor onto a blank diskette.

5.5 To Add a Volume Label to a Disk

You can assign a *volume label* (a name consisting of up to a maximum of 11
characters) to a diskette or a hard disk. A label gives you additional information to help you to identify the files on the diskette. When you display the
directory for the diskette, the volume label appears above the file names.
See the sample label, FRWINBOOK, in figure 5.2.

Volume label

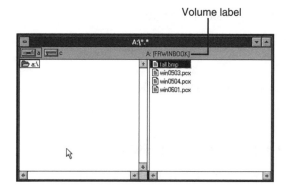

Fig. 5.2
An example
of a volume
label.

Use letters or numbers when labeling your diskettes because many special
characters are not allowed. In addition to the special characters not allowed in
file names (see Unit 4), you cannot use the following characters in label names:

(	opening bracket
)	closing bracket
&	ampersand
^	caret

Also, spaces cannot be used in a volume label. You can either label a diskette when you are formatting it, or you can add (or change) a label after the diskette is formatted. The following sections discuss both procedures.

Labeling a Disk While Formatting

To add a volume label to a diskette while it is being formatted, follow these steps:

1. Insert the diskette to be formatted into the disk drive.

2. Format the diskette by using the **Disk Format Disk** command from the File Manager window.

3. When the Format Disk dialog box appears, click inside the Label text box.

4. When the insertion point appears, type a volume label for the diskette.

5. Click OK, and then choose **Yes** to format the diskette.

6. The volume label is added to the diskette when it is formatted.

Adding a Label to a Formatted Diskette

You can add or change a volume label to a previously formatted diskette by following these steps:

1. Insert the formatted diskette into your floppy disk drive.

2. From the File Manager window, choose **Disk Label Disk**.

3. The Label Disk dialog box appears (see fig. 5.3).

Fig. 5.3
The Label Disk
dialog box.

4. Type the volume label into the Label text box.

5. If you are changing a volume label, highlight the existing label, and then type the new label.

6. Click OK.

7. The volume label is assigned to the diskette.

Exercise 3: Entering Volume Labels for Diskettes

In this exercise, you practice entering volume labels for a diskette.

1. Insert a formatted disk into your floppy disk drive.

2. From the File Manager window, select Disk Label Disk.

3. Type **classexer** into the Label text box, and click OK.

4. Change this label to **WINEXER**.

Unit Summary

This unit discussed the basics of using diskettes. You learned how to format a diskette, and how to make system disks. You also learned how to make a copy of a diskette. Finally, this unit showed you how to use a volume label to identify a formatted diskette more easily.

New Terms

To check your knowledge of the new terms in this unit, consult the glossary at the end of this book.

- Boot
- Diskette
- Floppy disk
- Formatting

6

Managing Files and Directories

Objectives

When you finish this unit, you will have learned the following:

6.1 To Set File Manager Confirmation Prompts

6.2 To Search for Files

6.3 To Select Files and Directories

6.4 To Copy Files

6.5 To Move Files

6.6 To Rename Files and Directories

6.7 To Delete Files and Directories

After learning the basics of the File Manager, you are ready to begin actual file management. Managing files includes locating needed files; copying, moving, and renaming files; and deleting files or directories.

All of these functions are necessary at one time or another for virtually every personal computer user. Learning how to perform these functions enables you to organize your hard disk and maintain control over your files. This unit covers the basic information you need to manage files and directories.

6.1 To Set File Manager Confirmation Prompts

It is important to remember that when you are moving or deleting file icons, you are moving and deleting actual files on your disk. Because it is easy to make a mistake and lose valuable information, you should turn on confirmation prompts when using the File Manager.

When confirmation prompts are turned on, Windows displays a dialog box confirming your action every time you want to copy, move, rename, or delete a file.

To set all of the confirmation prompts, follow these steps:

1. From the File Manager menu bar, choose Options Confirmation.

2. The Confirmation dialog box shown in figure 6.1 appears.

Fig. 6.1
The File
Manager
Confirmation
dialog box.

3. Check all the boxes in the dialog box, and then click OK.

As you become more familiar with File Manager, it is tempting to ignore the confirmation prompts. Don't! Take a few seconds to read any confirmation prompt you see to make sure you are doing what you really want to.

TIP

6.2 To Search for Files

Before you can use a file, you must locate it. The File Search option searches your disk for the file or files that you specify.

Use the File Search option to search for files when:

- You aren't sure what directory a file is in.
- You want to list all files with a specific extension.
- You need to list all file names that start with a certain letter or letters.
- You want to locate all files that contain specified letters within the file name.

Follow these steps to search for a file. You can use the mouse to click in each text box, or press `Tab⇥` to move from box to box.

STEPS

1. Choose File Search.

2. The Search dialog box appears (see fig. 6.2).

Fig. 6.2
The File Search
dialog box.

3. In the Search For text box, enter the name of the file you want to find. You can enter the entire file name, or use wild cards. (Wild cards are explained in the following section.)

4. In the Start From text box, enter the name of the directory from which you want the computer to start searching.

5. If you want to search all subdirectories of the directory from which the search is starting, select the Search All Subdirectories check box.

6. When all information in the dialog box is correct, choose OK.

7. The computer searches for the specified file. When the computer locates files matching the specifications, a Search Results window box appears, listing all of the matching files.

8. If no files are matched, a window appears with the message:
   No matching files were found.

Using Wild Cards to Search for Files

You can use *wild cards* to search for files. They are useful in locating all files with common characters in their names, or in locating a file if you are not sure of the exact spelling of the file name. A wild card is a character that takes the place of another character. There are two wild cards you can use: * and ?. The asterisk (*) takes the place of any number of characters. The question mark (?) replaces only one character.

For example, if you search for a file named WOR*.DOC, Windows lists all files that start with the letters WOR whether or not they have characters following, and end with the DOC extension.

If you enter the file name as WOR?.DOC, the files located begin with WOR, and have *only one character* (or no characters) after that, then a DOC extension.

The wild card *.* searches for files with any name and any extension, which is all the files on the disk.

Exercise 1: Searching for Files

Perform each of the following searches, using the File Search command. Notice which files you locate and why these files are selected.

1. Search for: calendar.hlp

   Start from: C:\
   Search all subdirectories

2. Search for: cal*.*

   Start from: C:\
   Search all subdirectories

3. Search for: cal?.hlp

   Start from: C:\windows
   Do not search all subdirectories

4. Search for: *.*

   Start from: c:\windows
   Do not search all subdirectories

6.3 To Select Files and Directories

Before you can copy, move, rename, or delete a file, you have to select the file you want.

To select a file using a mouse, follow these steps:

1. Position the pointer on the file you want.

2. Click the left mouse button. The file you selected is highlighted.

If you select the wrong file, you can deselect it by following these steps:

1. Move the mouse pointer to the file that is highlighted.

2. Click the left mouse button. The file is no longer selected.

The following sections of this unit provide you with instructions on copying, moving, renaming, and deleting a selected file.

6.4 To Copy Files

Copying a file creates an exact duplicate of the file in a different location, such as in a different directory or on a different disk. You can also make a duplicate of the file in the same directory, with a different name. Some of the reasons that you use the copy command are:

- When you need a copy of a file in a different directory.
- When you want to copy a file onto a diskette to give to someone else, or to have as a backup.
- When you want to copy a file from a diskette onto your hard disk.

Before you copy a file, you need to open the directory window where the file is currently located. Also, you need to make sure you can see the drive or directory to which you want to copy the file, either as an icon or an open window. This text instructs you to open the destination directory into a window to make it easier to copy the file to the correct location.

STEPS To copy a file to a different directory or subdirectory using the mouse, follow these steps:

1. Open the subdirectory containing the file you want to copy. In a second window, open the subdirectory where you want to place the duplicate.

2. Select the file you want to copy.

3. Hold down Ctrl and the left mouse button.

4. While continuing to hold down Ctrl and the left mouse button, drag the file to the new window.

5. When the file icon is in the location to which you want it copied, release the mouse button, then release Ctrl.

6. A confirmation dialog box appears, asking you to confirm the copy.

7. Check to make sure that you are copying the correct file and that it is going into the correct drive and directory. If both are okay, choose Yes.

8. If the file is not being copied to the correct directory, choose No. The copy command is cancelled.

9. If you choose the Yes command button, a duplicate copy of the file is placed in the new location.

 STEPS If you want to place a copy of the file in the same directory with a different name, follow these steps.

1. From the File Manager window, select the file you want to copy.

2. Choose **File Copy** from the menu bar.

3. The copy dialog box appears. Type the new name of the file in the **To:** text box.

4. Choose OK. A duplicate of the file is made under the new name you specified.

Exercise 2: Copying a File

Complete the following exercise to practice copying a file.

1. Insert into drive A, the formatted diskette you used in Exercise 1 in Unit 4.

2. Using the instructions in Unit 4, open windows for drive C and drive A.

3. Tile the windows so that they are displayed side by side on your screen.

4. After the windows are open, use the appropriate steps to copy the CALENDAR.HLP file from the WINDOWS subdirectory on drive C to the WINCLASS subdirectory on drive A.

6.5 To Move Files

If you *move* a file, the file is relocated to a different directory or drive. After you move a file, it no longer exists in its original location, only in the new location.

To move a file to another directory or subdirectory using the mouse, follow these steps:

STEPS

1. Open the subdirectory containing the file that you want to move. In a second window, open the subdirectory where you want to place the file.

2. Select the file you want to move.

3. Hold down both ⇧Shift and the left mouse button.

4. Drag the file to its new location.

5. When the file icon is in the correct drive and directory, release the mouse button, then release ⇧Shift.

6. A confirmation dialog box appears, asking you to confirm the file move.

7. Read the dialog box to make sure that you are moving the correct file, and that it is going to the correct drive and subdirectory. If both are okay, choose Yes.

8. To cancel the move command, choose the No command button.

9. If you choose Yes, the file is moved to the new location.

Exercise 3: Moving Files

Practice moving a file by completing the following exercise.

1. Make sure you have two windows open in File Manager: one for the root directory (\) on drive C, and another for the WINCLASS subdirectory on drive A.

2. Move the CALENDAR.HLP file from A:\WINCLASS to C:\.

Exercise 4: Copying and Moving More Files

Because copying and moving files is an integral part of file management, complete the following exercise for more practice at copying and moving files.

1. Copy the following files from C:\WINDOWS to the root directory on your diskette (A:\):

> HONEY.BMP
> LEAVES.BMP
> REDBRICK.BMP

2. Move the files you just copied from the root directory on your diskette (A:\) to the WINCLASS subdirectory (A:\WINCLASS). You need to open an additional window in order to display the WINCLASS subdirectory.

6.6 To Rename Files and Directories

After you have created a file or a directory, you may need to change its name. The *Rename* command changes the name of the file or directory without changing its location.

 STEPS

To rename a file, follow these steps:

1. Select the file or directory you want to rename.

2. Choose the menu option File Rename.

3. The Rename dialog box appears (see fig. 6.3).

Fig. 6.3
The Rename
dialog box.

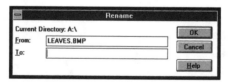

4. The From text box displays the name of the selected file.

5. Enter the new name for this file or directory into the To text box, and then choose OK.

6.7 To Delete Files and Directories

If you *delete* a file or directory, it is removed from your disk. When using the delete command, be careful not to delete a file or directory that you want to keep.

 Windows enables you to delete a subdirectory even if there are still files and subdirectories in it. Windows prompts you to confirm the deletion of each file in the subdirectory before it deletes the actual **WARNING** directory itself. Pay close attention to these confirmation prompts so that you don't accidentally delete a file you want to keep.

To delete a file or directory, follow these steps:

1. Select the file or directory you want to delete.

2. From the menu bar, choose File Delete.

3. The Delete dialog box appears enabling you to confirm which file or directory you are deleting (see fig. 6.4).

Fig. 6.4
The Delete dialog box.

4. Verify both the directory and file name. If they are correct, choose OK.

5. If you are deleting a directory that contains files, a dialog box appears for you to verify each file to be deleted. Verify the file name, and if you want to delete the file, choose the Yes command button.

6. If you are *absolutely certain* that you want to delete all of the files in the subdirectory, you can choose the Yes to All command button to delete all of the files without being prompted for each one.

7. If you decide that you do not want to delete the subdirectory, choose Cancel.

Exercise 5: Renaming and Deleting Files

Complete the following exercise to practice renaming and deleting files.

1. Rename LEAVES.BMP on your diskette to FALL.BMP.

2. Rename file HONEY.BMP on your diskette to MOLASSES.BMP.

3. Delete the CALENDAR.HLP file from C:\.

4. Delete the subdirectory WINCLASS on your diskette. Confirm each file deletion separately.

Unit Summary

This unit discussed setting confirmation prompts in order to confirm file copying, renaming, and deleting. You learned to select and deselect files and directories. You learned to copy, to move, and to rename files and also how to delete files and directories.

New Terms

To check your knowledge of the new terms in this unit, consult the glossary at the end of this book.

- Copy
- Delete
- Move
- Rename
- Wild cards

Testing Your Skills 2

(Units 4-6)

The following exercise is provided for you as a self-check to make sure that you understand the concepts and procedures presented to this point. If you have forgotten how to do something, refer back to the sections of this book which pertain to that subject. You will need two formatted diskettes to complete this exercise.

1. Open the File Manager program.

2. Open windows for the following disk drives and directories:

   > C:\WINDOWS
   > C:\DOS
   > A:\

3. Tile these windows.

4. Create the following subdirectories on the A:\ drive:

   > A:\CLASSEXE
   > A:\CLASSEXE\JANUARY
   > A:\WINTRAIN

5. Copy any two files from the C:\WINDOWS directory to A:\CLASSEXE.

6. Copy any file from C:\DOS to A:\.

7. Move a file from the A:\CLASSEXE subdirectory to A:\WINTRAIN.

8. Search for all files with an .EXE extension on C:\DOS only.

9. Delete the A:\CLASSEXE subdirectory and its file(s).

10. Copy this diskette to another by using the Copy Disk command.

11. Give the diskette a volume label. Use your name as the volume label.

12. Close the windows and the File Manager program.

The Help System

7

In using the Windows program, you may have noticed the **Help** menu option. You may also have noticed that some dialog boxes contain a Help command button. Windows has an extensive help system which can provide you with information about a task that you are performing, or how to complete a dialog box that you are using. The Help system also enables you to search for other help topics.

This unit discusses using the Help system. These same Help system concepts can be applied throughout all Windows programs.

Help System Overview

To access the Help system, select the **Help** option from the menu bar, or press F1. When you select Help from the menu bar, the menu shown in figure 7.1 appears.

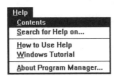

Fig. 7.1
The Help
menu.

Table 7.1 lists and briefly describes each of the available Help menu options.

Objectives

When you finish this unit, you will have learned the following:

7.1 To Use the Contents Option

7.2 To Use Jumps in Order to Display Help Information

7.3 To Search for a Specific Help Topic

7.4 To Use Bookmarks

Table 7.1 Help Menu Options	
Option	*Description*
Contents	Displays a list of the Help topics available in this window.
Search for Help on	Enables you to search for Help information on a specific topic. This option is discussed in detail later in this unit.
How to Use Help	Gives you information on how the Help system works.
Windows Tutorial	Enables you to use the Windows tutorial for a brief overview of the Windows program.
About (Program Manager)	Displays a window giving general information about the specific program that you are currently using. This information can include the version number, the copyright date, the developer, and to whom the software is licensed. The About option also shows you the percentage of system resources that are free, which indicates the amount of memory that is available.

The following sections present more detailed instructions on using some of these options.

7.1 To Use the Contents Option

The Contents option displays a list of Help subjects available for the program in which you are working.

STEPS

To display the Contents Option window, choose Contents from the Help menu, or press F1. The window shown in figure 7.2 appears on-screen.

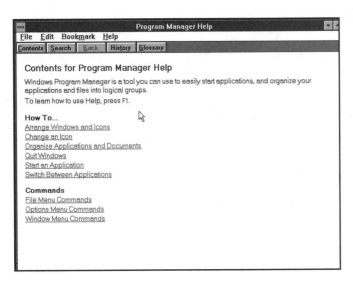

Fig. 7.2
The Contents
Window for
Program Manager
Help.

A menu bar is displayed at the top of the Help window. Five option buttons
are located below this menu bar:

Contents	Displays the available choices of Help topics for this program.
Search	Searches for help on a specific topic.
Back	Takes you back to the previous Help screen. If the button is gray, the option is not available.
History	Displays a window listing all of the Help screens you have selected during this Windows Help session.
Glossary	Displays a list of terms used in the Windows program. To see a particular term's definition, point to the term and click the left mouse button. You can use the scroll bars to scroll through all of the terms in this window.

A list of Help topics available for this application is located in the main section
of the window. If all of the topics do not fit in the window, vertical scroll bars
appear on the right side of the window.

To select a topic in a Help Contents window, follow these steps:

STEPS

1. Move the mouse pointer to the topic you want. Note that the mouse
   pointer turns into a pointing hand.

2. When the hand is positioned on the topic you want, click the left
   mouse button.

3. Information on the topic that you select is displayed.

4. To display the Help Contents window again, click the **Contents** option button.

Exercise 1: Using the Help Contents Option

Complete the exercise below to practice using the Contents option of the Help system.

1. From the Program Manager window, choose **Help Contents**.

2. Select each of the following help topics.

> Change an icon
>
> Start an Application
>
> Window Menu Commands

3. When you are back at the Contents window, select the **Back** command button. What window do you see? Why?

4. Select the **History** command button. A list of all of the Help screens you have accessed in this Windows Help session is displayed.

5. Close this window.

6. Close the Program Manager Help window.

7.2 To Use Jumps in Order to Display Help Information

When you are reading information about a topic that you have selected, you may notice a word or phrase with a solid or broken underline. This word is called a *jump*. If the jump has a solid underline, selecting it displays a new Help topic. When you select a broken-underlined jump, Help displays a definition of the term in a pop-up box.

Whenever you position the mouse pointer over a jump, the mouse pointer turns into a pointing hand. See the example in figure 7.3.

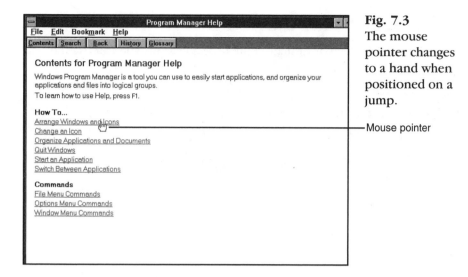

Fig. 7.3
The mouse
pointer changes
to a hand when
positioned on a
jump.

—Mouse pointer

To select a Jump complete these steps:

STEPS

1. Position the mouse pointer on the jump you want.

2. Click the left mouse button.

Exercise 2: Using Jumps

To practice using jumps in the Help system, complete this exercise.

1. Open the Help menu from the Program Manager window, and then choose Contents.

2. Select *Arrange Windows and Icons*. Notice that the phrase *title bar* is a different color and underlined with a broken line.

3. Position the mouse pointer on this phrase and click the left mouse button. A definition of this phrase appears in a pop-up box.

4. To remove the box, click the mouse button again.

5. Close the Help window.

73

7.3 To Search for a Specific Help Topic

If you want to locate Help information on a specific topic, you can use the Search option.

 STEPS To use the Search option, follow these steps:

1. Choose the Search option button from the Help window. A dialog box similar to the one shown in figure 7.4 appears.

Fig. 7.4
The Search dialog box in the Help window.

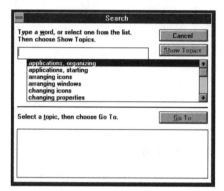

2. The list box displays a list of all of the available Help topics for this application. To see additional options, use the scroll bars, or type into the text box the first letter or two of the option you want.

3. Highlight the option you want. The text box displays the option's name.

4. Choose the Show Topics command button. The list box at the bottom of the window displays any topics related to the option you selected.

5. To see additional information on one of these topics, highlight the topic and select Go To.

Exercise 3: Using the Search Feature

In this exercise, you practice using the Help system Search feature.

1. Open the Write program.

2. Choose Help by pressing F1.

3. From the Contents menu, choose Search.

4. You want to see information on how to set margins, so type **m** in the text box. The list box appearance changes to show the first option that starts with the letter M.

5. The first option you see is *margins, setting*. Select this option.

6. The list box at the bottom displays the topic *Changing Page Layout*. Go To this topic.

7. Information on changing the page layout, which includes how to change margins, appears.

8. Close the Help window.

7.4 To Use Bookmarks

In using the Help feature, you may locate a Help screen that provides useful information that you want to access later. Instead of trying to remember exactly how you located the screen, you can insert a *bookmark* at the screen's location. This bookmark is similar to one you would use when reading a book: it marks a page of the Help system so you can easily locate it later.

To set a bookmark, follow these steps:

1. While the page you want to mark is displayed on-screen, choose the Bookmark option from the Menu Bar.

2. Select Define.

3. A dialog box appears (see fig. 7.5).

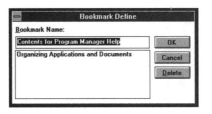

Fig. 7.5
The Bookmark
Define dialog box.

4. The text box displays the name that the Help system uses to refer to the topic currently in the Help window. You can change this name to anything you want, or leave it as it is. To change the name, just type a new name in the box.

5. When the bookmark is named, choose OK. A bookmark has been placed in this location.

6. When you select the Bookmark option again, a pull-down menu displays the bookmark name you just created. To go back to this Help page, click the name.

Exercise 4: Using Jumps and Defining Bookmarks

Complete this exercise to practice using the Help system and defining bookmarks.

1. Open the Write program, then choose **Help Contents**.

2. Select the jump *Change Paragraph Line Spacing*.

3. From this window, jump to *Formatting Paragraphs by Using the Ruler*.

4. Use the **Back** command button to return to the previous window.

5. Define a bookmark for this window and name it **Line Spacing**.

6. Use the **Search** option to show topics on *copying text*.

7. Go to the *Copying, Cutting, and Pasting Text* option.

8. Define a bookmark, and name it **Copying, Cutting, and Pasting Text**.

9. Use the **Book**mark option to locate the information on Line Spacing.

10. Open the History window to go to the Contents for Write Help window.

11. Exit the Help system.

12. Exit Write, and then the Accessories window.

Unit Summary

This unit discussed the basics of using the Help system. You learned to use the Contents option in order to locate help information, and to use jumps to display additional information. You also learned how to use bookmarks in order to refer to a specific Help screen.

New Terms

To check your knowledge of the new terms in this unit, consult the glossary at the end of this book.

- Bookmark
- Jump

Using the Print Manager

8

The Print Manager is a Windows utility that works in the background when you send a file to be printed. Most of the time you don't see the Print Manager, but there may be times when you need to access it in order to delete a print job, pause printing, or rearrange the order of the files to be printed. You also may need to access Print Manager in order to be able to print to a new printer, or to change your default printer.

8.1 To Print a File from a Windows Application

The exact steps to follow to print a file vary depending on which software package you are using; however, the basic procedure is the same. Use the following steps to print a document from the Write program.

Objectives

When you finish this unit, you will have learned the following:

8.1 To Print a File from a Windows Application

8.2 To Print a File from the File Manager

8.3 To Change the Order of Files to Be Printed

8.4 To Pause and Resume Printing

8.5 To Delete a File from the Print Queue

8.6 To Install a Printer

8.7 To Change the Default Printer

8.8 To Remove a Printer from the Installed Printers List

Unit 8: Using the Print Manager

STEPS To print a file from the Write program, follow these steps:

1. Open the Write application, and then the file you want to print.

2. From the menu bar, choose File **Print**.

3. A Print dialog box similar to the one shown in figure 8.1 appears. The exact dialog box you see depends on which software you are using and which printers you have installed.

Fig. 8.1
Write Print
Dialog Box.

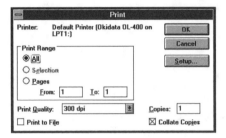

4. The name of the *default printer*, which is the printer to which Windows automatically prints, is displayed at the top of the dialog box. Choose the **Setup** command button to change any of the following printer options:

   - The printer
   - The printer orientation (portrait or landscape)
   - Paper size
   - Paper source (such as upper tray, manual feed, or envelope)

    In some programs, you may not be able to change the default
   NOTE printer at this point. If you need to change it, see the section "Changing the Default Printer" later in this unit.

5. After you have made any necessary printer changes, choose OK.

6. Choose any other available options in the Print dialog box, such as the range of pages, the print quality, and the number of copies.

7. Choose OK to send the file to the printer.

After the file has been sent to the printer, all of the information is sent to the Print Manager program. The Print Manager executes all of the printing details, and enables you to continue working while your file is being printed.

Exercise 1: Printing a File from Write

Complete the following exercise to print a file from the Write application.

1. Open Write, then open the CLASS1.WRI file, located on the disk provided by your instructor.

2. Choose File **P**rint.

3. From the Print dialog box, change Print **Q**uality to any one of the choices you have available, such as High or 300 dpi. Your choices vary depending on which printer you have installed.

4. Change the number of copies to 2.

5. Print the file.

8.2 To Print a File from the File Manager

In addition to printing a file from within a Windows application, you can also print a file from the File Manager. Using File Manager makes printing a file from a disk easier because you don't have to start the application and open the file.

To print a file from File Manager, follow these steps:

STEPS

1. Open File Manager and choose the file you want to print.

2. From the menu bar, choose File **P**rint.

3. A Print dialog box appears. Verify that you are printing the correct file, and then choose OK.

4. Depending on the type of file that you are printing, you may see another print dialog box. For example, if you are printing a Write file from the Program Manager, the Write Print dialog box appears. Choose the appropriate options.

5. The file is sent to the Print Manager.

8.3 To Change the Order of Files to Be Printed

When you send several files to the printer, they are arranged in a print *queue*, or list. The first file you send is printed first, the second is printed next, and so on. After you have sent several files to the printer, you may realize that you need to print the last file you sent before the other files.

Unit 8: Using the Print Manager

To change the order of the files (also called *print jobs*) in the queue, you need to access the Print Manager.

 STEPS

To open the Print Manager window, follow these steps:

1. Double-click the Print Manager icon that is displayed at the bottom of your desktop.

2. If you do not see the Print Manager icon, open the Main program group icon from the Program Manager window, and then open Print Manager.

3. The Print Manager window appears (see fig. 8.2).

Fig. 8.2
The Print
Manager.

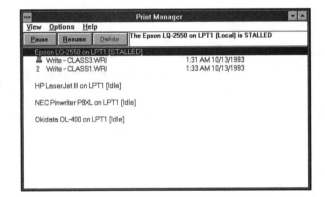

4. All installed printers are listed in this window. Each of the files that you have sent to be printed is listed under the printer name, in the order that it was sent to the printer.

 STEPS

To change the order of the print queue, follow these steps:

1. Highlight the print job that you want to move.

2. Hold down the left mouse button. The mouse pointer changes to a thicker arrow.

3. Drag the print job to the new location. When you see a dotted line around the area where you are moving the job, release the mouse button.

4. The file you selected is repositioned in the queue.

8.4 To Pause and Resume Printing

If you need to pause printing in order to correct a problem, follow these steps:

STEPS

1. In the Print Manager window, highlight the printer that you need to pause.

2. Choose the **P**ause command button. The printing stops until you restart it.

3. After you have paused printing, you need to choose **R**esume, from the Print Manager window, to start printing again.

    NOTE

    You also need to choose **R**esume if Print Manager has stopped the printing because of a problem with the printer.

If Print Manager cannot print your file, an error message similar to the one shown in figure 8.3 appears.

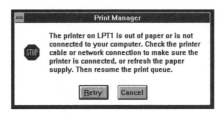

Fig. 8.3
A Print Manager printing error message.

After you have corrected the problem, go into Print Manager and choose the **R**esume command button.

NOTE

Do not try to print another copy of the file. It will not print until **R**esume is chosen for the Paused printer.

8.5 To Delete a File from the Print Queue

You may accidentally send a file to print and then want to cancel it before it prints. For instance, you may think of a change you want to make, or you may have requested 100 copies when you only wanted 10. Use the Print Manager to delete a print job.

81

Unit 8: Using the Print Manager

 STEPS   To delete a file from the print queue, follow these steps:

1. Open the Print Manager window.

2. Select the job you want to delete.

3. Click the **Delete** command button.

4. A confirmation box appears asking you to confirm that you want to stop the printing of the file.

5. Verify the file name. If it is correct, choose OK.

Exercise 2: Working with the Print Queue

Complete the following exercise to practice printing files and working with the print queue. Your instructor has copied files onto your diskette for you to use to practice printing.

1. Open the File Manager program from the Main program group. Make sure your windows are not maximized so you can see the desktop at the bottom of your screen.

2. Display a directory of your diskette.

3. Print 100 copies of the CLASS1.WRI file.

4. As soon as you see the Print Manager icon appear at the bottom of your desktop, open it and pause the printing.

5. Print 1 copy of each of these files:

    CLASS2.WRI
    CLASS3.WRI

6. Go back to the Print Manager.

     You may need to use the Task List to locate the Print Manager
    TIP window.

7. Move the CLASS3.WRI file in front of CLASS2.WRI. When you finish arranging them, they should be in this order:

    CLASS1.WRI
    CLASS3.WRI
    CLASS2.WRI

     You cannot move any file if it has already started printing.
    NOTE

8. Delete CLASS1.WRI from the queue.

9. Select your printer and resume printing, so that the other jobs print.

10. Close the Print Manager and File Manager windows.

8.6 To Install a Printer

When your Windows software was installed, a *printer driver*, which is a file that contains information about the printer you are using, should also have been installed. At some point, you may need to change this information, for instance, if you get a new printer, the wrong printer information was entered during the set up, or if a printer was not specified when the software was loaded.

To install a new printer, you must first install the printer driver, and then select the port to which the printer is assigned.

To install a new printer-driver file, follow these steps:

STEPS

1. Access the Print Manager program.

2. From the Print Manager menu bar, choose **Options Printer** Setup.

3. A dialog box similar to the one shown in figure 8.4 appears. This dialog box indicates which printer is the default printer, and shows all the other printers that are installed.

4. To install a new printer, choose the **Add** command button. A list box displays all of the printers supported by Windows.

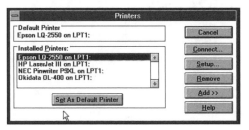

Fig. 8.4
The Printers
dialog box

5. Scroll through the list to locate the printer you want to install.

6. Highlight the name of the printer you want to install and choose the **Install** command button.

7. If the printer driver for the selected printer has not been installed, a dialog box appears prompting you to insert a specified Windows installation diskette. Insert the diskette into the drive indicated, and choose OK.

8. After the information is copied from the diskette to your hard disk, choose the Close command button from the Printers dialog box.

After installing the printer driver, you may need to select a different *printer port*, which is the connection device on the back of the computer into which you plug the printer cables. The two types of ports used are *LPT* and *COM*. An LPT port is a *parallel port*, used only for printers. A COM port is a *serial port*, which means it can be used for various devices including a modem, a printer, or a mouse. A printer generally uses the LPT port.

The system assigns your printer to port LPT1, which is the first parallel port. If you have more than one parallel port and want to assign the printer to a different one, or if you are setting up a serial printer, you need to change the printer port.

Follow these steps to change the printer port:

1. From the Printers dialog box, highlight the name of the printer for which you want to change the port.

2. Choose Connect. The Connect dialog box shown in figure 8.5 appears.

Fig. 8.5
The Connect
dialog box.

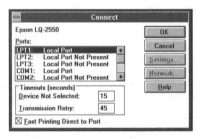

3. Highlight the port that you want to select. If the list indicates that a particular port is not present, this port is not available on your PC.

4. Choose OK. The port for this printer is changed.

Exercise 3: Installing a Printer Driver, and Changing the Printer Port

Practice installing a printer driver and changing the port by completing the following exercise.

1. Use the appropriate steps to install the Epson FX-85 printer.

2. When the system prompts you to insert an installation diskette, choose Cancel so the printer driver is not installed on your computer.

3. Highlight one of your installed printers in the list box near the top of the Printers dialog box.

4. Choose the Connect command button.

5. Select a different port from the list box, then click the OK button.

6. Choose Connect again, and change the port back to the original.

7. Close the Printers dialog box, and then close the Print Manager.

8.7 To Change the Default Printer

The *default printer* is the printer that Windows automatically uses, unless you specify a different one. When you looked at the Printers dialog box in the previous section, you saw which printer was currently designated as the default printer. If this printer is not the one you normally use, you need to change this default.

Follow these steps to change the default printer:

1. Open Print Manager and choose Options Printer Setup.

2. The Printers dialog box appears. You can change your default printer to any of the printers listed in the Installed Printers list box.

3. Select the printer you want to use as the default, and then click the Set As Default Printer command button.

4. Choose Close.

Exercise 4: Changing the Default Printer

Complete this exercise to practice changing your default printer.

1. Follow the previous steps to change your default printer to any printer in the Installed Printers list box.

2. Set your default printer back to the original printer.

8.8 To Remove a Printer from the Installed Printers List

If you are no longer using a printer, you may want to remove it from the list of Installed Printers.

 STEPS

To remove a printer from the Installed Printers list, follow these steps:

1. Open Print Manager and choose **Options Printer** Setup.

2. The Printers dialog box appears. Highlight the printer you want to remove.

3. Choose the **Remove** command button.

4. A confirmation dialog box is displayed. If you have selected the correct printer to be removed, choose **Yes**.

5. Choose Close to close the Printers dialog box.

Exercise 5: Installing a Printer Driver, Changing the Default Printer, and Removing a Printer

Complete the following exercise to practice installing a printer driver, changing the default printer, and removing a printer.

1. Your instructor will tell you which printer to install. Install this printer using the instructions stated earlier in this unit. If the system prompts you to enter a Windows diskette and you do not have access to Windows system diskettes, choose Cancel at this window.

2. Select the printer you just installed, and change the port to COM1.

3. Note which printer is currently your default printer.

4. Change your default printer to the printer you just installed.

5. Remove this printer.

6. Since this printer is removed, you have no default printer. Select the printer that was originally your default, and set it as the default printer.

Unit Summary

In this unit, you learned how to print files from Windows applications and from the File Manager. You learned to use the Print Manager to control the print queue by changing the order of printing, pausing and resuming printing, and deleting a print job. You also learned to use Print Manager to add a different printer to your system, to change the default printer, to change the printer port, and to remove a printer that you are no longer using.

New Terms

To check your knowledge of the new terms in this unit, consult the glossary at the end of this book.

- Default printer
- Landscape
- Parallel port
- Portrait
- Print jobs
- Printer port
- Printer-driver file
- Queue
- Serial port

9

Objectives

When you finish this unit, you will have learned the following:

9.1 To Access the Control Panel

9.2 To Change the Screen Saver

9.3 To Change the Wallpaper for Your Desktop

9.4 To Change your PC's Date and Time

9.5 To Change Mouse Settings

9.6 To Use the Clock

9.7 To Create and Delete Program Groups

Using the Control Panel and Creating Group Icons

Windows includes options to customize the way Windows looks on your screen. The Control Panel enables you to make various modifications including changing the Screen Saver, the Wallpaper, and the date and time, as well as modifying some of your mouse settings. Windows also enables you to display a clock on your screen, and to customize the group icons that appear in the Program Manager window.

9.1 To Access the Control Panel

To access the Control Panel, follow these steps:

 STEPS

1. From the Program Manager window, select the Main icon, and then the Control Panel icon.

2. The Control Panel window, shown in figure 9.1, appears.

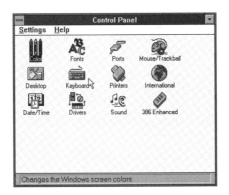

Fig. 9.1
The Control Panel
window.

9.2 To Change the Screen Saver

When your computer has been idle for a certain period of time, Windows displays a *screen saver*. A screen saver is a varying pattern which keeps the monitor from being damaged by motionless characters displayed on-screen for a long period of time. To go back to the screen in which you were working when the screen saver became active, just press any key.

Windows enables you to choose from various screen savers, and you can also determine the amount of time your computer is idle before the screen saver is activated.

To change the screen saver, follow these steps:

1. From the Control Panel, select the Desktop icon. The Desktop dialog box, shown in figure 9.2, appears.

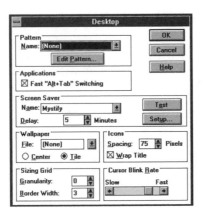

Fig. 9.2
The Desktop
dialog box.

2. The screen saver information is in the third box from the top of this window. To change the screen saver pattern, click the down arrow in the Name drop-down list box.

3. A list of the screen savers from which you can choose is displayed. Select the screen saver you want to use.

4. To preview this screen saver, choose the Test option button. The screen saver appears.

5. Press any key to go back to the dialog box.

6. To change the number of minutes your computer is idle before the screen saver becomes active, type the number of minutes in the Delay text box, or click one of the arrows. Click the up arrow to increase the number of minutes, or click the down arrow to decrease the number of minutes. You can choose from 1 to 99 minutes.

7. Select OK to save your settings.

9.3 To Change the Wallpaper for Your Desktop

Wallpaper is the background pattern on your desktop. When you first load Windows, the background is light gray. You can "wallpaper" your desktop with various patterns including cars, castle bricks, and tartan plaid. You can also use drawings that you create with the Paintbrush application.

 STEPS

To change the wallpaper on your desktop, follow these steps:

1. From the Control Panel, select the Desktop icon. The desktop dialog box appears (refer to figure 9.2).

2. Click the down arrow in the File drop-down list box within the Wallpaper box. A list of all available wallpaper options is displayed.

3. Use the scroll bars to move through the list to locate the wallpaper you want. If you have created any Paintbrush files, they also are displayed in this list.

4. Highlight the wallpaper you want to use.

5. Choose the Center option button to center this pattern in the middle of your screen. If you want to Tile the pattern across your desktop, choose Tile.

Most of the wallpaper options look best when tiled. Tiling displays many of the items across the screen. Use Center if you have created a Paintbrush file that you are using and want only one item to be displayed on your desktop.

6. Choose the OK command button to save your selection. The wallpaper you selected is displayed on your desktop.

 Wallpaper patterns use a great deal of memory. If Windows is running slowly and you need more available memory, change the wallpaper pattern to None.

Exercise 1: Changing the Screen Saver and the Wallpaper

Complete the exercise below to practice changing the screen saver and the wallpaper.

1. Open the Control Panel icon, and then the Desktop icon as outlined in previous steps.

2. Change the screen saver to Starfield Simulation with a delay of one minute.

3. Change the wallpaper to Egypt, and tile it.

4. Click the OK command button.

5. You will see the wallpaper you selected on your desktop. Do not touch your keyboard or mouse for one minute to see the screen saver you selected.

6. After you have viewed the screen saver, press any key to return to your screen.

9.4 To Change Your PC's Date and Time

Your computer keeps track of the date and time. This is useful because the date and time are stored with any files that you save. Some programs also enable you to automatically insert the current date and time in a file.

Usually, the date and time will be maintained by your computer, but it is a good idea to check them periodically and change them if necessary. Also, you may need to change the time if you go on daylight savings, or if you have to install a new battery in your computer.

91

STEPS

If you are running Windows from a server, you cannot change the date and time. The server's timer is in control.

To change the date and time, follow these steps:

1. From the Control Panel, select the Date/Time icon. The Date & Time dialog box appears (see fig. 9.3).

Fig. 9.3
The Date and
Time dialog box.

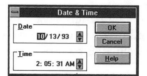

2. To change the date, press [Tab⁺] to move to the part of the date you want to change (month, day, and/or year) and type the correct number.

3. Press [Tab⁺] to move down to the time. Press [Tab⁺] to move to the numbers you want to change, and then type the correct time.

4. After you have corrected the date and time, choose OK.

Exercise 2: Changing the Date and Time

Practice changing the date and time by completing the following exercise.

1. Change the date to August 6, 1993.

2. Change the time to 3:43:38 p.m. You will correct the date and time in a later exercise.

9.5 To Change Mouse Settings

You may need to change mouse settings in order to change the speed of your double-clicks, or to swap the left and right mouse buttons. The following sections give you detailed instructions on making these changes.

Changing the Double-Click Speed

If you find you are having trouble double-clicking at the correct speed for your computer, you can change Windows double-click speed setting.

To change the double-click speed of your mouse, follow these steps: **STEPS**

1. From the Control Panel, open the Mouse icon.

2. The Mouse dialog box, shown in figure 9.4, appears.

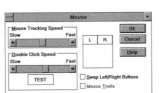

Fig. 9.4
The Mouse dialog box.

3. Move the mouse pointer to the scroll bar labeled **Double Click Speed**.

4. To make your double-clicks slower, move the scroll box to the left. If you are double-clicking too fast, move the scroll box to the right.

> ⚠️ Do not move the scroll box all the way to the right when changing the double-click speed. You will not be able to double-click
> **WARNING** fast enough to make it work.

5. Double-click the TEST box to see if your double-click speed is correct. If you double-click at the appropriate speed, the box becomes highlighted.

6. When the double-click speed is set correctly, choose OK.

Swapping Left and Right Mouse Buttons

If you are left-handed, you may want to swap your mouse's left and right buttons. This enables you to maneuver the mouse with your left hand and click the right button with your index finger to make various selections in the Windows program. When you swap these buttons, all references to the left mouse button actually refer to the right mouse button.

To swap the right and left mouse buttons, follow these steps: **STEPS**

1. Open the Mouse icon in the Control Panel window.

2. The Mouse dialog box appears (refer to fig. 9.4).

3. Click the check box labeled Swap Left/Right Buttons.

4. Choose OK to save your changes and exit this window.

If you swap the mouse buttons, you must click with the right mouse button to choose OK, or to remove the check from the check box.

Exercise 3: Changing Mouse Settings

Complete the following exercise to change the mouse settings.

1. Open the Mouse window from the Control Panel.

2. Change your double-click speed, making it slightly slower than the current setting.

3. Select the Swap Left/Right Buttons check box. Now you have to click your right mouse button to select options.

4. Click the OK command button with the right mouse button.

Exercise 4: Making Changes in the Control Panel

This exercise gives you additional practice at making changes in the Control Panel. You also change the left mouse button, and the date and time back to their original settings.

1. Access the Mouse icon in the Control Panel. Remember you have to click with the right mouse button.

2. Click the Swap Left/Right Buttons check box to remove the X.

3. If you need to, change the double-click speed.

4. Click the OK button to close this dialog box.

5. Open the Desktop window.

6. Change the screen saver settings to the following:

   Mystify
   5 minute delay

7. Change the wallpaper settings to the following:

   Marble.bmp
   Tile

8. Choose OK in the Desktop dialog box.

9. Open the Date & Time window and change the date and time to the correct information.

10. Choose OK to close this box, and then close the Control Panel and Main windows.

9.6 To Use the Clock

The Windows program contains a clock that continuously displays the current time based on the computer's internal timer. You can display this clock on your desktop, if you want.

To display Windows' clock on your desktop, follow these steps: *STEPS*

1. Open the Accessories group icon from the Program Manager, then open the Clock icon. A clock window appears.

2. You can change the way the clock is displayed by using the Settings menu. Choose settings to display the Settings pull-down menu. See figure 9.5 for an example of this menu.

Fig. 9.5
The Clock Settings menu.

3. To change the clock so that it appears as an analog clock, choose the Analog option. To display a digital clock instead, choose Digital from the menu.

4. Choose the Set Font option to change the font in which the digital clock is displayed.

5. If you choose No Title, the window title and menu bar are not displayed. To redisplay the title, double-click the clock window.

6. To display a second hand on the analog clock, or seconds in digits on the digital clock, choose the Seconds option.

7. You can display the date by choosing the Date option. The digital clock displays the date under the time. The date on the analog clock appears in the title bar.

After you have changed the clock settings, you may want the clock to be displayed on your screen at all times.

 STEPS

To display the clock icon on-screen at all times, follow these steps:

1. Minimize the clock window. It appears as an icon at the bottom of the desktop.

2. To make sure this icon does not get covered when you open additional windows, click once on the clock. This displays the clock control box menu.

3. Choose Always on Top from this menu. Even if other windows move to the same location on your desktop, the clock icon will always be visible.

Exercise 5: Using the Clock

You practice using the clock in this exercise.

1. Open the clock icon.

2. Open the Settings menu. Click each of the following options so that a check mark appears next to it.

   Digital
   Seconds
   Date

3. Minimize the window.

4. Make the clock always appear on top of any windows displayed on your desktop.

9.7 To Create and Delete Program Groups

Windows organizes applications on your computer into *groups*. These are represented by the group icons you see in the Program Manager window. Each group icon contains program-item icons for your applications. When Windows is installed, it automatically creates several groups, including Applications, Main, and Games. When you add more Windows software, other groups may be automatically created.

You can also create additional groups of applications. This can be helpful if you have several applications you use regularly, and you want their program-item icons located in the same group window.

Creating a New Program Group

To create a new group, follow these steps.

1. From the Program Manager window, choose File New. The New Program Object dialog box appears (see fig. 9.6).

Fig. 9.6
The New Program Object dialog box.

2. Choose the Program Group option button, then click OK.

3. The Program Group Properties dialog box, shown in figure 9.7, appears.

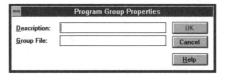

Fig. 9.7
The Program Group Properties dialog box.

4. Type a name for the group icon in the Description text box, then click OK. This name is the group icon label, and appears under the icon in the Program Manager window.

5. A program group window appears.

Adding an Application to a Program Group

After you have created a new program group, you are ready to add the applications. An application must be installed on your computer before you can add it to a program group. Adding an application to a program group is not the same as installing a new application; it just includes a program-item icon in a particular group window.

To add an application to a Program Group, follow these steps:

1. Open the Group window to which you want to add the application.

2. From the Program Manager window, choose File New. The New Program Object dialog box appears.

3. Choose the Program Item option, and then click OK.

4. The Program Item Properties dialog box appears (see fig. 9.8).

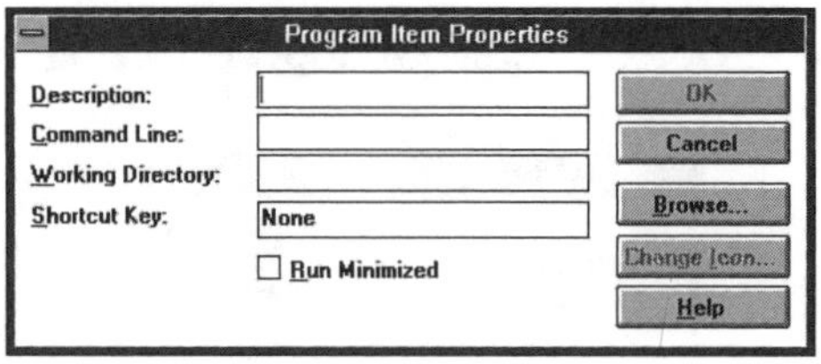

Fig. 9.8
The Program Item
Properties dialog
box.

Program Item Properties

Description:

Command Line:

Working Directory:

Shortcut Key: None

☐ Run Minimized

OK

Cancel

Browse...

Change Icon...

Help

5. In the Description text box, type the name you want to appear as the program-item icon label.

6. In the Command Line text box, type the path and executable file name used to start this application. If you do not know the application's executable file name, look in the program documentation. Executable file names usually have an .EXE extension.

   As an example, the Write application is usually located in the WINDOWS subdirectory. The executable file name is WRITE.EXE. To add this application to the program group, type the following in the Command Line text box:

   C:\WINDOWS\WRITE.EXE

7. If you want a different default directory used while you are working in the application, type the name of that directory in the Working Directory text box.

8. To start the application as an icon instead of in a window, choose the Run Minimized check box.

9. Choose OK. The program-item icon is added.

   If you have entered information incorrectly, you will see a dialog box telling you what information is wrong. Select the program-item icon, then the File Properties option from the Program Manager window to correct the problem.

Exercise 6: Creating Program Groups and Adding Applications

To practice creating a program group and adding an application, complete the following exercise.

1. Execute the necessary steps to open the Program Object dialog box and select Program Group.

2. Use your name followed by the word Applications to name the program group icon. For example, Michele's Applications.

   Choose OK.

3. A program group window appears.

4. Choose File New from the Program Manager window.

5. Choose the Program Item option, and then click OK.

6. In the Description text box, type **Write**.

7. In the Command Line text box, type **C:\WINDOWS\WRITE.EXE**. If the Write application is located in a different subdirectory on your PC, your instructor will tell you what to enter here.

8. Choose OK. The Write program-item icon appears in the window.

9. Test the application by opening this icon.

10. Close the application window and the group window.

To Delete an Application from a Program Group

You also can delete a program-item icon in a program group. This does not delete the application, but just the icon representing the application in the group window.

To delete an application from a Program Group, follow these steps:

STEPS

1. Open the group window where the application is located.

2. Select the program-item icon.

3. From the menu bar, choose File Delete.

   TIP
   You can also select the icon, and just press ⌐Del⌐.

4. A dialog box appears asking you to confirm the deletion. If you want to delete the item, choose **Yes**. To cancel the deletion, choose **No**.

5. If you choose **Yes**, the icon is removed from the group window. The application program is still on your disk, so you can add this application to another group window.

To Delete a Program Group Icon

You can delete an entire Program Group icon as well. If the program group contains program-item icons, they will be deleted at the same time.

 To delete a program group, follow these steps:

1. Select the group icon you want to delete from the Program Manager window.

2. From the menu bar, choose File Delete, or just press ⌑Del⌑.

3. You are prompted to confirm the deletion of this group. Choose Yes if you want to delete this group, or No to cancel the deletion.

Exercise 7: Deleting Application and Program Group Icons

The exercise below lets you practice deleting application and program group icons.

1. Open the group window you created in Exercise 6.

2. Delete the Write program-item icon.

3. Close the Group window.

4. Delete this program group icon.

Unit Summary

In this unit, you learned how to use the Control Panel to change the screen saver and wallpaper settings. You learned how to change the mouse options in order to make it easier to use. You also learned how to use the clock and how to make the clock always be displayed on your desktop. The final section explained how to create and delete program groups.

New Terms

- Screen saver
- Wallpaper

Testing Your Skills 3

(Units 7-9)

The following exercise is provided for you as a self-check to make sure that you understand the concepts and procedures presented to this point. If you have forgotten how to do something, refer back to the sections of this book which pertain to that subject.

1. Open the Print Manager. Select **Help** **C**ontents.

2. Select the jump *Print Your Documents*.

3. Select *Changing the Print Order*.

4. Display the jump *local printer*. Remove the definition display from your screen.

5. Define a bookmark for this screen and name it **Print Order**.

6. Go back to the previous help screen.

7. Use the History button to return to the Contents for Print Manager Help window.

8. Print this screen.

9. Exit Help and Print Manager.

10. Open the Control Panel.

11. Change the Screen Saver and Wallpaper to any pattern you want.

12. Close the Control Panel.

13. Open the Accessories icon and the Clock.

14. Change the clock to analog.

15. Close the Accessories window.

16. Add a program group named **Daily Work**.

17. Copy the following applications to this group:

> Paintbrush
> Notepad
> Calendar

18. Delete the entire program group.

Glossary

Active window. The window you are currently using. The active window's title bar is highlighted.

Application icon. The icon that appears when you have opened and minimized a program or file.

Application window. A window that contains a program you are running, for example a window containing a Write file or a Paintbrush document.

Bookmark. Marks a specific Help screen so that you can easily refer to it later.

Boot. To turn on the computer.

Clipboard. An area of your computer's memory that stores information you have cut or copied from a Windows document. You can paste information stored in the Clipboard into another Windows document.

Copy. A command that duplicates a file from one disk or directory to another, or makes a duplicate of the file in the same directory, but with a different name. After completing the copy command, two copies of a file exist.

Default printer. The printer your PC uses unless you specify a different one. In Windows, you set the default printer by using the Print Manager program.

Delete. Removing, or erasing, a file from a disk.

Desktop. The background area on your screen, behind any windows that you have open.

Dialog box. A box that appears in a window when Windows needs you to specify more information. Windows displays dialog boxes when executing commands such as opening files, printing files, and changing window options.

Directory. A section of your disk that enables you to store related files together. Directories are given names using the same rules as file names.

Disk. A permanent storage area, usually inside of your PC.

Disk drive. A secondary storage medium which holds the disk and hardware needed to write information to a disk. You have a hard disk drive inside your PC, which is referred to as drive C. You may also have one or two floppy disk drives, which hold diskettes. The first floppy disk drive is drive A, the second is drive B.

Diskette. A small, removable disk used to store files and programs. Also called a floppy disk.

File. A collection of data, such as a letter or spreadsheet.

File name. A name given to a collection of data. File names must follow DOS naming conventions.

Floppy disks. A small, removable disk used to store files and programs. Also called a diskette.

Formatting. Preparing a diskette to store files. Formatting erases any information currently on the disk, divides it into sectors, and creates a File Allocation Table (FAT) to keep track of the information stored in each sector.

Graphical User Interface (GUI). An operating system that uses pictures and graphics to represent programs and files.

Group icon. An icon that is displayed in the Program Manager window. It contains other icons used to start various programs. Examples of group icons include Games and Accessories.

Group window. A window containing icons that start applications. A group window is opened when you open a group icon such as Accessories, Main, or Games, from the Program Manager.

Icon. A picture that represents a program or file. You can select an icon to open a program such as Write, or to copy a file in the File Manager program.

Insertion point. A blinking vertical line that is displayed when you type information. Any text you type is entered at this line.

Jump. A term or phrase that you select in the Help system to display additional information.

Landscape orientation. The rotation of a page design to print text and/or graphics horizontally across the longer axis of the page.

Memory. Temporary work area used by the computer whenever you load a program or file. When you turn off your computer, any information that hasn't been saved to a disk is removed from memory.

Menu bar. A bar displayed along the top of most windows which lists program options from which you can choose. You select a menu bar option in order to display a listing of related options.

Move. Taking an item from one disk or directory and putting it in a new location. When you move a file, only one copy exists.

Parallel port. A port that is used only for printers. Also identified as an LPT port.

Parent directory. The directory immediately above the current directory.

Portrait orientation. The default printing orientation for a page of text, with the longest measurement oriented vertically.

Print jobs. Files that you sent to the printer.

Printer driver. A file that contains information about your printer. This file is installed when you set up your printer.

Printer port. The slot on the back of your PC into which you plug the printer.

Program-item icon. An icon that represents a program. These icons appear when you open a group icon.

Queue. The list of files waiting to print. Files are listed in the order that you send them to the printer.

Rename. Changing the name of a file. When you rename a file, it no longer exists under its old name.

Screen saver. A moving pattern that displays on your screen after your PC is idle for a period of time. Because the pattern moves, it prevents any characters from being permanently burned into the screen on your monitor.

Scroll bars. Bars that appear along the side or bottom of a window when more information exists in a window than can be displayed. Arrows within the scroll bars are used to move through the window in order to display the additional information.

Glossary

Serial port. A port that can be used for printers, modems, or a mouse. It is also identified as a COM port.

Subdirectory. A directory below the current directory.

Wallpaper. A pattern that you can select to display on your desktop.

Wild card. A character that takes the place of another character in a file name. Two wild cards are available in Windows: * takes the place of any number of characters; ? replaces only one character.

Index

A

About (Program Manager) command
(Help menu), 70
accessing
Control Panel, 88
File Manager, 42
active window, 33, 103
All File Details command (File
Manager, View menu), 48
analog clock, 95
applications, *see* programs
Arrange Icons command (Program
Manager, Window menu), 27

B

bookmarks, 75-76, 103
booting computers, 52, 103
buttons
command, 21
Maximize, 11
Minimize, 9-11
mouse
switching left and right, 93-94
option, 22-23
Restore, 11

C

Cascade command (Program
Manager, Window menu), 26-28
cascading windows, 25-26
in Task List, 30-33
check boxes, 22-23
Clipboard, 34, 103
Edit menu commands, 36
contents, viewing, 34
clocks, 95-96
closing windows, directory, 45-46
COM ports, 84
command buttons, 21
command-line interface, 2
COMMAND.COM file, 52
commands
Bookmark menu, Define, 75
Clipboard Edit menu
Copy, 36
Cut, 35
Paste, 36
File Manager
Disk Copy Disk, 54-55
Disk Format Disk, 51-53, 56
Disk Label Disk, 56
Disk Make System Disk, 53
File Copy, 62-63
File Create Directory, 44

File Delete, 65-66
File Exit, 47
File Print, 79
File Rename, 64
File Search, 59-61
Options Confirmation, 58
View All File Details, 48
View By File Type, 48
View Directory Only, 48
View Name, 48
View Partial Details, 48
View Sort By Name, 48
View Split, 48
View Tree and Directory, 48
View Tree Only, 48
File menu, Print, 78-79
Help menu
About (Program Manager
menu), 70
Contents, 70, 76
How to Use Help, 70
Search for Help on, 70, 74-75
Windows Tutorial, 70
Print Manager
Delete, 82-83
Pause, 81
Printer Setup, 85-86
Resume, 81
Program Manager
File Delete, 99-100
File New, 97-100
Help/How to Use Help, 18
Window Arrange Icons, 27
Windows Cascade, 26-28
Windows Tile, 27
computers
booting, 52
clock, 95-96
dates/times, 91-92
Confirmation dialog box, 58
confirmation prompts, 58-59

Connect dialog box, 84
Contents command (Help menu),
70-72, 76
Control Panel
accessing, 88
dates/times, 91-92
mouse settings, 92-95
screen savers, 89-91
wallpaper, 90-91
Copy command (Clipboard, Edit
menu), 36
Copy command (File Manager, File
menu), 62-63
Copy dialog box, 62
Copy Disk command (File Manager,
Disk menu), 54-55
copying, 34, 103
files, 61-64
floppy disks, 54-55
text to Clipboard, 35-36
Create Directory command (File
Manager, File menu), 44
Create Directory dialog box, 44
Cut command (Clipboard, Edit
menu), 35
cutting, 34
text to Clipboard, 35-36

D

dates/times, 91-92
default printers, 78, 85, 103
deleting, 86
Define command (Bookmark
menu), 75
Delete command (File Manager, File
menu), 65-66
Delete command (Print Manager),
82-83
Delete command (Program
Manager, File menu), 99-100
Delete dialog box, 65

deleting, 103
   directories, 65-66
   files, 65-66
      print, 81-83
   printers from Installed Printers
   list, 86
   program group icons,
    96-100
Desktop, 4, 103
   screen savers, 89-91
   wallpaper, 90-91
Desktop dialog box, 89
destination disks, 54-55
dialog boxes, 104
   components, 18-19
      check boxes, 22-23
      command buttons, 21
      list boxes, 20-21
      option buttons, 22-23
      text boxes, 19-21
   Confirmation, 58
   Connect, 84
   Copy, 62
   Create Directory, 44
   Delete, 65
   Desktop, 89
   Format Disk, 51, 56
   Label Disk, 56
   Mouse, 93-95
   New Program Object, 97-100
   Options, 23
   Print, 23, 78-79
   Printers, 84-86
   Program Group Properties,
    97-100
   Rename, 64
   Search, 59
digital clock, 95
directories, 43, 104
   creating, 44-45
   deleting, 65-66

displaying, 47
   parent, 105
   renaming, 64-66
   root, 42-43
   types, 41-42
Directory Only command (File
  Manager, View menu), 48
directory trees, 44
disk drives, 1, 41, 104
   displaying, 44
   floppy, 41
   icons, 43
Disk menu commands (File
  manager)
   Copy Disk, 54-55
   Format Disk, 51-53, 56
   Label Disk, 56
   Make System Disk, 53
Disk Operating System, *see* DOS
diskettes, *see* floppy disks
disks, *see* floppy disks; hard disks;
  system disks
DOS (Disk Operating System), 1-2
   terms, 40-42
double-clicking speed, 92-93
dragging and dropping, 7
drivers, installing printer, 83-85
drives, *see* disk drives
drop-down list boxes, 20-21

E

Edit menu commands (Clipboard)
   Copy, 36
   Cut, 35
   Paste, 36
Exit command (File Manager, File
  menu), 47
exiting
   File Manager, 47
   Task List, 29-30
   Windows, 11-12

F

FATs (File Allocation Tables), 51
file icons, 43
File Manager, 2
  accessing, 42
  commands
    Disk Copy Disk, 54-55
    Disk Format Disk, 51-53, 56
    Disk Label Disk, 56
    Disk Make System Disk, 53
    File Copy, 62-63
    File Create Directory, 44
    File Delete, 65-66
    File Exit, 47
    File Print, 79
    File Rename, 64
    File Search, 59-61
    Options Confirmation, 58
    View All File Details, 48
    View By File Type, 48
    View Directory Only, 48
    View Name, 48
    View Partial Details, 48
    View Sort By Name, 48
    View Split, 48
    View Tree and Directory, 48
    View Tree Only, 48
  confirmation prompts, 58-59
  directories
    creating, 44-45
    displaying, 47
    windows, opening/closing,
      45-46
  drives, displaying, 44
  exiting, 47
  View menu, 47
  window components, 42-44
File menu commands (File
  Manager)
  Copy, 62-63
  Create Directory, 44
  Delete, 65-66

Exit, 47
Print, 79
Rename, 64
Search, 59-61
File menu commands (Program
  Manager)
  Delete, 99-100
  New, 97-100
files, 41, 104
  copying, 61-64
  deleting, 65-66
  finding, 59-61
  moving, 63-64
  naming, 41, 104
  printing
    from File Manager, 79
    from Windows programs,
      77-79
    order, 79-80
    pausing/resuming, 81
  program, 43
  renaming, 64-66, 105
  saving to disk, 9
  selecting, 61
finding
  files, 59-61
  Help topics, 70-71, 74-75
floppy disks, 41, 104
  care and maintenance, 50-51
  copying, 54-55
  formatting, 51-54
  volume labels, 55-57
Format Disk dialog box, 51, 56
formatting, disks, 104
  floppy, 51-54
  system, 52-54
  volume labels, 56-57

G-H

glossary, Help Contents window, 71
graphical user interface, *see* GUI
graphics
    copying/moving to Clipboard,
      34-36
    selecting, 35
group icons, 10, 104
group windows, 104
    arranging, 25-28
groups, program, creating/deleting,
    96-100
GUI (graphical user interface),
    2, 104

hard disks, 41
    organizing, 42
    volume labels, 55-57
Help menu commands (Program
    Manager)
    About, 70
    Contents, 70-72, 76
    How to Use Help, 18, 70
    Search for Help on, 70, 74-75
    Windows Tutorial, 70
Help system, 69-70
    bookmarks, 75-76
    jumps, 72-73, 76
How to Use Help command
    (Program Manager, Help menu),
    18, 70

I

I-beams, 35
icons, 2, 104
    arranging, 27-28
    Desktop, 89-90
    disk drive, 43
    file, 43
    group, 104
    moving, 7

program, 103
    Task List window, 32-33
program-item, 26, 105
    selecting with mouse, 6-7
    types, 10
insertion points, 104
installing printer drivers, 83-85

J-L

jumps, Help system, 72-73, 76, 105

Label Disk command (File Manager,
    Disk menu), 56
Label Disk dialog box, 56
landscape orientation, 78, 105
list boxes, 20, 21
LPT ports, 84

M

Make System Disk command (File
    Manager, Disk menu), 53
Maximize button, 11
memory, 9, 105
menu bars, 16-18, 105
menus, selecting options, 16-18
Minimize button, 9-11
mouse, 6-7
    buttons, switching, 6, 93-94
    dragging and dropping, 7
    settings, 92-95
    windows
      opening/closing, 7
      resizing, 8, 9
Mouse dialog box, 93-95
moving, 105
    files, 63-64
    icons/windows, 7

N-O

Name command (File Manager,
    View menu), 48

naming files, 41, 104
   see also renaming
New command (Program Manager,
   File menu), 97-100
New Program Object dialog box,
   97-100

opening
   directory windows, 45-46
   Print Manager, 80
   Task List, 28-30
option buttons, 22-23
Options dialog box, 23
Options menu commands (File
   Manager), Confirmation, 58
orientation, printers, portrait/
   landscape, 78, 105

P

paper (printing), size/source, 78
parallel ports, 84, 105
parent directories, 105
Paste command (Clipboard, Edit
   menu), 36
pasting, 34
Pause command (Print Manager), 81
portrait orientation, 78, 105
ports
   parallel, 84, 105
   printer, 84-85, 105
   serial, 84, 106
Print command (File Manager, File
   menu), 79
Print command (Windows
   programs, File menu), 78-79
Print dialog box, 23, 78-79
print jobs, deleting from queue,
   81-83, 105
Print Manager, 77
   commands
      Delete, 82-83
      Options Printer Setup, 85-86

Pause, 81
   Resume, 81
Printer Setup command (Print
   Manager, Options menu), 85-86
printers
   default, 78, 85, 103
      deleting, 86
      installing, 83-85
   ports, 84-85, 105
Printers dialog box, 84-86
printing files
   from File Manager, 79
   from Windows programs, 77-79
   order, 79-80
   pausing/resuming, 81
program files, 43
   COMMAND.COM, 52
Program Group Properties dialog
   box, 97-100
program groups, creating/deleting,
   96-100
program icons, 10, 103
   arranging, Task List window,
      32-33
Program Manager
   Accessories, Clock, 95
   commands
      File Delete, 99-100
      File New, 97-100
      Help/How to Use Help, 18
      Window Arrange Icons, 27
      Windows Cascade, 26-28
      Windows Tile, 27
   Control Panel, 88
   groups, creating/deleting, 96-100
   window components, 3-6
   Window menu, 25-26
program windows, 103
   open, listing, 28-32
program-item icons, 10, 26, 105
   Windows, printing from, 77-79
prompts, confirmation, 58-59

Q-R

queues, print, 80, 105
 files, deleting, 81-83

Rename command (File Manager, File menu), 64
Rename dialog box, 64
renaming, 105
 directories, 64-66
 files, 64-66
resizing windows, 8-9
Restore button, 11
Resume command (Print Manager), 81
root directories, 42-43
 see also directories;
  subdirectories

S

saving files to disk, 9
screen savers, 89-91, 105
scroll arrows, 15
scroll bars, 14-16, 105
scroll boxes, 15
Search command (File Manager, File menu), 59-61
Search dialog box, 59
Search for Help on command (Help menu), 70, 74-75
searching, *see* finding
selecting
 files, 61
serial ports, 84, 106
shaded menu options, 17
Sort By Name command (File Manager, View menu), 48
source disks, 54-55
Split command (File Manager, View menu), 48
subdirectories, 42-43, 106
 see also directories; root
  directories

system disks, creating, 52-54
 when formatting, 53
 with Disk menu, 53

T

Task List, 28
 application icons, arranging, 32-33
 exiting, 29-30
 opening, 28-30
 windows
  cascading/tiling, 30-33
  closing, 29-30
  switching, 29-30
text
 Clipboard
  copying/moving , 34-36
  cutting, 35-36
 selecting, 34-35
text boxes, 19-21
Tile command (Program Manager, Window menu), 27
tiling windows, 25-27
 Task List, 30-33
times/dates, 91-92
Tree and Directory command (File Manager, View menu), 48
trees, directory, 44

U-V

utilities
 Print Manager, 77
 see also programs

View menu, options, 48
View menu (File Manager), 47
 options
  All File Details, 48
  By File Type, 48
  Directory Only, 48
  Name, 48
  Partial Details, 48

Sort By Name, 48
Split, 48
Tree and Directory, 48
Tree Only, 48
volume labels, disks, 55-57

W-Z

wallpaper, 90-91, 106
wild cards, 106
  finding files, 60
Window menu (Program Manager), 25-26
Window menu commands (Program Manger)
  Arrange Icons, 27
  Cascade, 26-28
  Tile, 27
Windows
  advantages, 2-3
  exiting, 11-12
  starting, 3
windows
  activating, 33
  active, 103
  cascading, 25-26
    Task List, 30-33
  directory
    opening/closing, 45-46
  File Manager
    components, 42-44
    directory displays, changing, 47
  group, 104
    arranging, 25-28
  maximizing, 11-12

minimizing, 10-11
moving, 7
opening/closing, 7
program, 103
  open, listing, 28-32
Program Manager components, 3-6
resizing, 8-9
tiling, 25-27
  Task List, 30-33
Windows Tutorial command (Help menu), 70

NOTES

NOTES

NOTES

NOTES

NOTES

NOTES